How I Got Over

Healing for the African American Soul

R. Neal Siler

How I Got Over: Healing for the African American Soul
Published by New Life Publishing

Copyright © 2010 by R. Neal Siler

ISBN 978-0-9883012-0-7

Printed in USA

All rights reserved. No part of this book may be reproduced or transmitted in any form or by any means without written permission from the author. All rights reserved. No part of this book may be reproduced or transmitted in any form or by any means without written permission from the author.

Unless otherwise indicated, Bible quotations are taken from The King James Version (KJV) and The New International Version (NIV).

For Information:
New Life Publishing
A Ministry of New Life Ministries of Virginia, Inc.
804.730.1348

Dedication

To Sharon and our children, Jonathan and Kirsten whom I love without limits, you are such inspiration to me. Without you I could not be complete and I would not know the joys of this journey to wholeness.

To Mom and Dad, everyday thoughts of you awaken a new inspiration within me and I realize you are my greatest gift. Thank you.

TABLE OF CONTENTS

Preface	7
Introduction	13
Chapter One: Your Journey To Wholeness	23
Chapter Two: If God Loves Me Then Why…? *Overcoming Barriers to God's Love.*	33
Chapter Three: It's So Hard For Me To Trust	43
Chapter Four: Lord I Hurt	59
Chapter Five: Who Told You That?	69
Chapter Six: Michael's Story	81
Chapter Seven: No One Really Cares About My Feelings	99
Chapter Eight: Singing In A Minor Key	113
Chapter Nine: When Home Is Where Your Heart Is Broken	125
Chapter Ten: How Deep Is This Well?	135
Chapter Eleven: What You See In The Mirror *Image and Identity*	149
Chapter Twelve: Let The Church Say Amen	159
Chapter Thirteen: How Did We Get Here? *Healing is not Supposed to Hurt*	171
Chapter Fourteen: The Source of Truth	185
Chapter Fifteen: Why Must I Forgive – Can't I Just Say I'm Sorry?	197
Chapter Sixteen: Obedience and Death *The Way of the Cross*	221

Preface

In Alan Callahan's *The Talking Book: African Americans and the Bible*, he opens the section entitled "Emmanuel" with the following quote by Howard Thurman.[2]

To some he is the grand prototype of all the distilled longing of mankind for fulfillment, for wholeness, for perfection. To some he is the Eternal Presence hovering over all the myriad needs of humanity, yielding healing for the sick of body and soul, giving a lift to those whom weariness has overtaken in the long march, and calling out hidden purposes of destiny which are the common heritage. To some he is more than a Presence; he is the God fact, the Divine Moment in human sin and human misery. To still others he is a man who found the answer to life's riddle, and out of a profound gratitude he becomes the man most worthy of honor and praise. For such his answer become humanity's answer and his life the common claim.

There are many African Americans who are successful and live model lives. From these individuals we draw hope, and dream dreams of our own potential and possibilities for success. In the black community, we all know black families or even black heroes whose lives reveal hurt and brokenness.

Their experiences and bad decisions represent the "gloomy clouds of night" looming over the lives of many African Americans. Whether we talk about a superstar athlete who, from the looks of things, has everything going for him, or the everyday person that we see at work, at church or talk to on the phone, there is a thread of pain and brokenness that reveal our deep human need for God's love.

We are a hurting people. And often, out of our pain, we hurt each other. African Americans comprise 13.5% of the U.S. Population, yet 43% of all murder victims in 2007 were African American, 93.1% of whom were killed by another African American.[1] Government data will show that 62% of all black households are single parent homes, that one out of nine young Black men between the ages of 18 and 34 are incarcerated. Data will also show that 23% of all African Americas are living at 100% below the poverty level, representing 12.7% of Black men 18-64 and 21.5% of black women of the same demographic. Also, 57.5% of all African Americans in a family of two live at 300% below the poverty level.[2] We most often do not connect the data with the despair that is deeply felt by many African Americans whose lives are reflective of these statistics.

The data does not show the hurt, the loss, the pain, or the feelings of hopelessness within the lives

---

[1] 2007. Center for healing hearts and Spirits. Black on Black Crime Brochure. Little Rock, Arkansas

[2] Bella Online, *The Voice of Women* http://www.bellaonline.com/articles/art8507.asp

of those who make up the statistics. It does not show the bondage of pain passed on from one generation to the next. Wanting respect, but not knowing how to earn it. Wanting to succeed, but finding success is illusive because "society won't give us a chance". And in many instances, when we are successful, forget the one thing that forever unites us – black skin. So in many instances we hurt one another because we see in each other what we do not like about the larger society who has yet to affirm our giftedness. And, the ills perpetrated upon us, as a people of color are still very real. We cannot undermine the sinister and seditious forces of racism – in many respects benign because of the perceived advances of society. But, yet very much, an insidious cancer, that erupts as an unsuspecting malignancy.

From August 27, 2005 to September 5, 2008, in an AP-Yahoo News poll conducted with Stanford University, 2,227 adults were surveyed regarding their feelings and views about African Americans. One third (1/3) of the whites polled, all democrats, harbored negative views of black people. What is very telling about this survey is that it was to be a gauge of the potential success of Barack Obama's presidential campaign bid as our nation's first African American President. This was a survey of the members of his own party. With a margin of sampling error of plus or minus 2.1 percentage points, the poll sought to measure latent prejudices among whites about blacks. More than a quarter of white Democrats agree that "if blacks would only try harder, they could be just as well off as whites."

The survey also incorporated images of black and white faces to measure implicit racial attitudes and prejudices that are more deeply rooted than people realize that have them. The incidence of racial prejudice in this case was even higher, with more than half of whites revealing more negative feelings toward blacks than whites. Further, negative adjectives were often used to describe blacks, such as "violent", "boastful", "complaining", "lazy", and "irresponsible." Whites were more likely to "stay on the fence" when asked to give a word that would be a positive assessment. MSNBC's reporting of the survey, concluded with the remarks of John Clouse, a 57 year old white male gathered at a coffee shop in Somerset, Ohio, speaking on behalf of himself and his friends ... "We still don't like black people."[3]

The shadows of pain that loom over us as an African American people are often minimized, played down and disregarded. It is as if it is expected that our days are to be filled with dark clouds. In our efforts to make the best of things we do pretty well, most of the time. But, then, there are those moments where something happens and we do not have it all together. We emerge from the shadows – from behind our mask long enough to feel deeply, our pain. In those moments, we glance at that which hurts us and most often strike out at others, hurting them, usually

---

[3] http://www.msnbc.msn.com/id/26803840/ns/politics-decision_08

the ones we love most, because we do not want to face our brokenness. We do not have the heart equipment on board to absorb it. We don't know what to do with it. So we lash out hoping to bury it again and pray that it will haunt us no more. But it does. In a matter of time, we will face it again and with each successive visit we become more embittered and more hostile, more determined to not hurt – but we do.

It is the goal of this work to mine the pain, to dig into the well that is so deep and draw to the surface that which mars and hides our true selves. That which keeps us from being free to really love and to be loved in the way that we want to be loved – authentically, truly as the gift that we are, must be discovered.. Created by a God who loves you immeasurably, you are invited into this journey. It is a God encounter, where you will find answers to many of life's questions; rest for your weariness; and above all, healing for your soul.

How I Got Over

How I got over, How did I make it over
You know my soul look back and wonder
How did I make it over
But, soon as I can see JESUS
The man that died for me
Man that bled and suffered
and he hung on Calvary

And I want to thank him for how he brought me
And I want to thank GOD for how he taught me
Oh thank my GOD how he kept me
I'm gonna thank him 'cause he never left me

Then I'm gonna thank GOD for 'ole time religion
and I'm gonna thank GOD for giving me a vision
One day I'm gonna join the heavenly choir
I'm gonna sing and never get tired

And then I'm gonna sing
somewhere 'round GOD'S altar
And I'm gonna shout all my troubles over
You know I've gotta thank GOD and thank him for
being so good to me. 'LORD YEAH'

- Mahalia Jackson

Introduction

After the Egyptian and Indian, the Greek and Roman, the Teuton and Mongolian, the Negro is a sort of seventh son, born with a veil, and gifted with second-sight in this American world, – a world which yields him no true self-consciousness, but only lets him see himself through the revelation of the other world. It is a peculiar sensation, this double-consciousness, this sense of always looking at one's self through the eyes of others, of measuring one's soul by the tape of a world that looks on in amused contempt and pity. One ever feels his twoness – an American, a Negro; two souls, two thoughts, two unreconciled strivings; two warring ideals in one dark body, whose dogged strength alone keeps it from being torn asunder.

The history of the American Negro is the history of this strife, – this longing to attain self-conscious manhood, to merge his double self into a better and truer self. In this merging he wishes neither of the older selves to be lost. He would not Africanize America, for America has too much to teach the world and Africa. He would not bleach his Negro soul in a flood of white Americanism, for he knows that Negro blood has a message for the world. He simply wishes to make it possible for a man to be both a Negro and an American, without being cursed and spit upon by his fellows, without having the doors of opportunity closed roughly in his face.

This, then, is the end of his striving: to be a co-worker in the kingdom of culture, to escape both death and isolation, to husband and use his best powers and his latent genius. These powers of body and mind have in the past been strangely wasted, dispersed, or forgotten. The shadow of a mighty Negro past flits through the tale of Ethiopia the Shadowy and of Egypt the Sphinx. Through history, the powers of single black men flash here and there like falling stars, and die sometimes before the world has rightly gauged their brightness.[4]

I read DuBois' *The Souls of Black Folk,* in my college days when I was idyllically Black. It was the early seventies. I was a student at the University of North Carolina – Chapel Hill. It was the crest of the civil rights era. Hopeful, filled with prism like dreams of achieving and being successful in any number of professions – the sky was the limit. I, gifted with promise and wonder. The world, wide open, it wasn't long before my kaleidoscope of dreams for fortune, success and acceptance met with a cold harsh reality. I neither had the key to, nor owned the door that granted access to my wishes, hopes, and dreams.

---

[4] DuBois, W.E. Burghardt, 1953. *The Souls of Black Folk: Essays and Sketches, p. 3.* New York: Bantam

I would soon discover that the world was not as welcoming, nor as friendly as I had believed. In fact, the world was often cruel – to the point of chocking the life out of even the best dream and igniting, instead of hope, a quietly seething anger – a petulance of sorts that created a discomfort, weariness, a disease over the reality that this was not going to be an easy journey. The, Negro, Colored, Black, African American, presence, long after the Civil War, long after the Equal Rights Amendments, long after Time Magazine's article that Africa is the cradle of civilization – whether discussing poverty, education, crime, music or sports – racism is still a fundamental issue in America.

I recall a PBS documentary in 2003 entitled *Race: The Power of Illusion.* In this documentary, anthropologists, biologists and geneticists found that, biologically speaking, there is no such thing as "race." Also, like beauty, they discovered that skin color is only skin deep. Nonetheless, the fact remains that race is deeply woven into the fabric of American life.

One of the most fascinating segments in the PBS documentary was Episode 3: "The House We Live In." This episode focused on how our country's social institutions create racial barriers by providing different groups with different life chances. Remember, this is 50 years after the Civil Rights Act. From the Documentary, quoting James Horton, Professor of American History, George Washington University,

> *Virginia law defined a Black person as a person with 1/16th African ancestry. Florida defined a black person as a person with 1/8th African ancestry. Alabama said, 'You are Black if you got any African ancestry at all.' But you know what this means? You can walk across a state line and literally, legally change race. Now what does race mean under those circumstances? You give me the power, I can make you any race I want you to be, because it is a social, political construction.*[5]

In 1894, Mark Twain wrote the classic *Pudd'n Head Wilson*, in which he tells the story of Roxana a young slave woman, fearing for her infant's son's life, exchanges her light-skinned child with her master's. Treating racial prejudice and slavery as the real criminals, Mark Twain offers this snapshot of the unfathomable pain of being black and the incredible prejudice that had to be endured. He writes,

> *To all intents and purposes Roxanna was as white as anybody, but the 1/16 of her that was black outvoted the other 15 parts and made her a Negro. She was a slave and saleable as such. Her child was 31 parts white and he too was a slave, and by a fiction of law and custom, a Negro.*[6]

These were extreme measures, even exhausting measures to guarantee the ostracism of a people group, namely African Americans. And so, the fallout from years of such ostracism, prejudice, and

---

[2] 2003. PBS Documentary, *Race: The Power of Illusion*
[3] Twain, Mark. 1984. *Pudd'n Head Wilson.* New York: Bantam

racism, clearly rooted in the American institution of slavery, has been the broken hearts, the broken spirits, and the untold emotional damage done to African Americans. The historical denial of access to opportunity, human rights, and the present subversive and covert forms of racism that are pervasive in culture, continue to re-open, and re-wound an already broken people.

Exodus Chapters 1 – 3 records the story of the children of Israel's Egyptian Bondage. While Joseph was alive, enjoying Pharaoh's favor, the Hebrews enjoyed prosperity in the paganism of Egypt. As they became 'a populous people' according to Exodus Chapter 1, the Egyptians became fearful of them and began to subdue them with harsh labor.

> *9 And he said to his people, "Look, the people of the children of Israel are more and mightier than we; 10 "come, let us deal shrewdly with them, lest they multiply, and it happen, in the event of war, that they also join our enemies and fight against us, and so go up out of the land." 11 Therefore they set taskmasters over them to afflict them with their burdens. And they built for Pharaoh supply cities, Pithom and Ramses. 12 But the more they afflicted them, the more they multiplied and grew. And they were in dread of the children of Israel. 13 So the Egyptians made the children of Israel serve with rigor. 14 And they made their lives bitter with hard bondage – in mortar, in brick, and in all manner of*

> service in the field. All their service in which they made them serve was with rigor (Exodus 1:6-14, NKJV).

These were God's 'chosen' people. Not only was God concerned about the injustice of their treatment, but God's heart was touched by their pain. When the Israelites were now burdened beyond hope, they cried out to God.

> 23 Now it happened in the process of time that the king of Egypt died. Then the children of Israel groaned because of the bondage, and they cried out; and their cry came up to God because of the bondage. 24 So God heard their groaning, and God remembered His covenant with Abraham, with Isaac, and with Jacob. 25 And God looked upon the children of Israel, and God acknowledged them (Exodus 2:23-25, NKJV).

There is an intriguing pattern in this predicament. It is a pattern of hope. Notice:

- They cried out because of their bondage
- Their cry came up to God, because of their bondage
- God heard their cry – their groaning
- God remembered His covenant
- God acknowledged their pain and suffering.

God hears the cry of His people. In the words of the Psalmist, "We are His people and the sheep of

His pasture" (Psalm 100:3 KJV). We have a right to cry out to him. He wants to hear and acknowledge our cry. He said to Moses, the would-be deliverer of the Hebrews,

> *7 And the LORD said: "I have surely seen the oppression of My people who are in Egypt, and have heard their cry because of their taskmasters, for I know their sorrows. 8 "So I have come down to deliver them out of the hand of the Egyptians, and to bring them up from that land to a good and large land, to a land flowing with milk and honey..." (Exodus 2:7, 8 NKJV).*

Even though it may seem like a long time coming, even though we may become entrenched in our pain and it feels like nothing will overcome our hurt, God is preparing us for a work of the heart – a work that will turn our hearts back to Him. For all the injustices that you may have experienced, from blatant prejudice and overt racism to broken trust and fractured familial relationships, God says, "I have heard your cry and am come now to deliver you to a good land." I so want that, for me, for you, for all those who have been marginalized and oppressed. For my African American brothers and sisters, who have been abused and abandoned – those who have suffered discrimination because of gender or denied access to opportunity because of "where you come from, what you look like, or what you do not have" –

God says, I hear your cry and I have come for you, to give you a good land.

This book is about inner-healing as taught in the formational prayer model pioneered by Dr. Terry Wardle. Formational prayer is a ministry of the Holy Spirit, moving through a Christian caregiver, bringing the Healing Presence of Jesus Christ into the place of pain and brokenness within a wounded person.[7] Formational Prayer offers life-changing pathways that help people dismantle destructive false beliefs, teaches steps for dealing with deep wounds, presents tools for addressing dysfunctional behaviors, provides a foundational understanding of trauma and the traumatized, and addresses spirituality and world view as each relates to helping the broken. Because of its emphasis on the individual's relationship to Christ and the dynamic of the Holy Spirit as the true healer, it is with this specific focus in mind that I address systemic, historical, and situational woundings that are so much a part of African American life.

As the pages of this volume unfold, I invite you to lay hold of the promise of Psalm 107:20, 21, "He sent forth his word and healed them; he rescued them from the grave. Let them give thanks to the LORD for his unfailing love and his wonderful deeds for men." May you claim and embrace for yourself, the principles of freedom and wholeness that I believe

---

[7] 2001. Wardle, Terry. *Healing Care, Healing Prayer*. Abilene, Texas: Leafwood Publishers

God is delivering to you. It is essential to your well being, and to the life of glorious joy and fulfillment that God has promised.

Shalom

Chapter One

Your Journey to Wholeness

The day that you were born heaven applauded your arrival. Those awaiting your arrival should have celebrated and really made over you! You were the gift waited for – the prize of the party. And, as you developed and grew the celebration should have continued. Given the proper loving nurture and structure you would have grown up in a friendly and inviting world. The sky would be the limit for you and you could accomplish anything you wanted to accomplish. No dream would be too big. No goal unattainable. That was the beginning of your journey. But what if you were born into a family that did not know how to create such a safe place for you?

That is how the journey began for many African Americans. We are born into families that on the surface appear to be loving and kind, and for the most part they are. While nice and caring in many ways, parents withhold themselves from their children, because they do not know anything else to do. They can only do what they know to do. They are not abusive to their children. They are not intentionally neglectful. They are passive in many ways but very demanding, authoritative and quick to discipline in other ways – usually ways that matter the most emotionally. Children work hard at getting their parents attention. Their parents, not knowing that their acting out is a cry for connecting, discipline more, structure more and distance themselves more. In the meantime, because they are uncertain and are not sure how to act around them, inside that child is craving for touch – to be held, to be loved, to be noticed, to be celebrated, to be attended, and made to feel special.

Our fathers and mothers can be well liked, even popular. They can give to causes, work hard in the church, pray fiery prayers that will call heaven down. But when it comes to creating a safe and secure environment where children can grow, thrive and become, they many times miss the mark. Never attuning, emotionally distant, withholding attention, sometimes caustic with each other, tuning each other out, turning each other off, children get the sense this is how life works.

The real truth is that most African American parents try hard to be good parents and to give their children the emotional gifts necessary to make life work. But there is so much that gets in the way, much of it purely a history of not knowing how. In an effort to protect themselves they create pain for each other, and certainly for their children. Mothers try harder most often taking on an inequitable share of responsibility in the home. Fathers become more passive and distant and even more disconnected from the children. Children grow up insecure, becoming susceptible to abusive relationships, inappropriate acting out and aberrance. Yet, not knowing does not prevent the fallout that comes into a child's life. Poorly equipped to navigate life successfully because they have been robbed of necessary life endowments, their parents' woundedness, creates wounds within themselves that forces them to live a compromised life of "broken treasures and lost dreams."

Life Application

You Can't Give It If You Didn't Get It

When actor Will Smith kissed his son Jaden on the lips it sparked a fury of blog responses. Some responses defended the actor's actions as a genuine act of love expressed towards his son, stating that many African American youngsters have never experienced loving affection from their fathers. Others described it as perverted and inappropriate suggesting that a father should never kiss his twelve year old son on the lips. Chronicles of the Smith's family's interactions portray both Will and Jada, as marvelously loving parents who not only appropriately share affection with their children, but create moments of enduring memories in the times they spend together, in the support and encouragement they provide.

In a 2002 Child Trends study on the significance of parental warmth and affection on wellbeing, 93% of white mothers, 76% of white fathers report hugging their child at least once a day and telling them on a regular basis that they are loved and appreciated. In this same study, 75% of black mothers and 45% of black fathers are likely to hug their child at least once a day or tell their child he or she is loved and appreciated on a regular basis. [8]

Historically, appropriate displays of love and affection have been a missing element in the fabric of most African American households. In conjecturing reasons as to why this is so, most sociologists trace this lack of parental warmth and affection in African American households to the effects of slavery on African American families. In 1965, during the Johnson administration, New York Senator, Daniel Patrick Moynihan, released a report entitled, *The Negro Family: The Case for National Action*.[9]

In reviewing the work of sociologist, E. Franklin Frazer[10], Moynihan traced the problems of the African American family back to slavery. Further, he concluded that slavery had left "a racist virus of unimaginable mistreatment in the American bloodstream," that has been perpetuated for over three centuries. Frazer describes this legacy as fostering the disintegration of poor, urban black families and the development of what Moynihan called a

---

[8] Child Trends. 2002. *Charting Parenthood: A Statistical Portrait of Fathers and Mothers in America*. Wash. DC, ,http://www.childtrends.org

[9] The Moynihan Report. Office of Policy Planning and Research. 1965. *The Negro Family: The Case For National Action*. United States Department of Labor

[10] E. Franklin Frazier. 1939. *The Negro Family in the United States* (Chicago: University of Chicago Press

"fatherless matrifocal (mother-centered) pattern" within black families where men did not learn roles of providing and protecting – a shortcoming passed down through generations.[11]

Even a cursory look at the impact of slavery suggests the degree to which many African Americans are handicapped in varying abilities to connect emotionally, to encourage, to love, to give what it takes for their offspring to realize their full potential as a human being that can walk through life successfully. Yet in the deepest part of our being, that God-birthed desire for love, nurture and place was always present as this advertisement placed in the *Colored Tennessean* newspaper in Nashville, Tennessee on October 7, 1865 attests.

> **Information Wanted.**
> INFORMATION is wanted of my mother, whom I left in Fauquier county, Va., in 1844, and I was sold in Richmond, Va., to Saml. Copeland. I formerly belonged to Robert Rogers. I am very anxious to hear from my mother, and any information in relation to her whereabouts will be very thankfully received. My mother's name was Betty, and was sold by Col. Briggs to James French.— Any information by letter, addressed to the Colored Tennessean, Box 1150, will be thankfully received.
> THORNTON COPELAND.
> sept16–3m

Original Ad.

---

[11] Herbert G. Gutman, *The Black Family in Slavery and Freedom, 1750-1925*.

INFORMATION is wanted of my mother, whom I left in Fauquier county, Va., in 1844, and I was sold in Richmond, Va., to Saml. Copeland. I formerly belonged to Robert Rogers. I am very anxious to hear from my mother, and any information in relation to her whereabouts will be very thankfully received. My mother's name was Betty, and was sold by Col. Briggs to James French.—Any information by letter, addressed to the Colored Tennessean, Box 1150, will be thankfully received.

THORNTON COPELAND

This young man searched for his mother. It is not known if Thornton Copeland or the other thousands of people who searched for family members ever found them. Yet one can imagine what it must be like to be torn from your mother, to not know her whereabouts for years – to wonder if she thinks about you or if she even makes similar inquires about your whereabouts. One can only guess at the degree of loss and emotional robbery.

In many instances African Americans were not permitted to be "family", to nurture, to create an experience of loving and being loved; to do so was often temporary and at great risk of deep emotional pain and loss. So in large measure "caring" was compromised and eclipsed by a system that did not care. And although there is a resiliency in us, seen in the fact that many slaves would create new families after their owners sold their original families apart, this fostered a sense of detachment and a belief that one should not get too connected, too close, or too possessive as one never knew when that which was so loved would be sold away or taken away.

Public Sale of Negroes,
By RICHARD CLAGETT.

On Tuesday, March 5th, 1833 at 1:00 P. M. the following Slaves will be sold at Potters Mart, in Charleston, S. C.

Miscellaneous Lots of Negroes, mostly house servants, some for field work.

Conditions: ½ cash, balance by bond, bearing interest from date of sale. Payable in one to two years to be secured by a mortgage of the Negroes, and appraised personal security. Auctioneer will pay for the papers.

A valuable Negro woman, accustomed to all kinds of house work. Is a good plain cook, and excellent dairy maid, washes and irons. She has four children, one a girl about 13 years of age, another 7, a boy about 5, and an infant 11 months old. 2 of the children will be sold with mother, the others separately, if it best suits the purchaser.

A very valuable Blacksmith, wife and daughters; the Smith is in the prime of life, and a perfect master at his trade. His wife about 27 years old, and his daughters 12 and 10 years old have been brought up as house servants, and as such are very valuable. Also for sale 2 likely young negro wenches, one of whom is 16 the other 13, both of whom have been taught and accustomed to the duties of house servants. The 16 year old wench has one eye.

A likely yellow girl about 17 or 18 years old, has been accustomed to all kinds of house and garden work. She is sold for no fault. Sound as a dollar.

House servants: The owner of a family described herein, would sell them for a good price only, they are offered for no fault whatever, but because they can be done without, and money is needed. He has been offered $1250. They consist of a man 30 to 33 years old, who has been raised in a genteel Virginia family as house servant, Carriage driver etc., in all which he excels. His wife a likely wench of 25 to 30 raised in like manner, as chamber maid, seamstress, nurse etc., their two children, girls of 12 and 4 or 5. They are bright mulattoes, of mild tractable dispositions, unassuming manners, and of genteel appearance and well worthy the notice of a gentleman of fortune needing such.

Also 14 Negro Wenches ranging from 16 to 25 years of age, all sound and capable of doing a good days work in the house or field.

Thus, for African American people slavery made family formation impossible. Since slaves could not marry, family life could not be stable or secure. Family separation through sale was a constant threat. Thus, it was not only African American mothers who were faced with the pain of forced separation from their families. Similarly, a father might have one owner and his wife and children another. And fathers were often sold away without regard to the fact that they had children. Equally, when fathers were not sold away, the ostracism and degradation was so shaming that it created another dynamic of pain and disenfranchisement. The pain that comes from being treated as a cipher or chattel took its toll on the African American male psyche.[12]

You can't give it if you didn't get it. Slaves were neither nurtured nor encouraged to thrive and grow in the way that was best for them. Slaves were property and their owners made stringent often times demeaning demands without regard to comfort, physical capacity or personal wellbeing. Disciplined severely and reprimanded harshly for the most part for not performing to "Masters" expectations. At some level it is easy to understand how such conditions could create a sense of apathy and detachment towards the very idea of family. It is out of this crucible that the African American family is spawned.

---

[12] The Moynihan Report. Office of Policy Planning and Research. 1965. *The Negro Family: The Case For National Action.* United States Department of Labor

Clearly, the impact of slavery on African American family formation is a source of pain and brokenness that many African Americans rarely connect with. It is not in our awareness. Perhaps because it is over one hundred years removed. But the mindset, the protective mechanisms employed for survival, and the effects of this evil reach far and deep into who we are as a people. It is openness to and awareness of this unconscious reality that can provide a pathway to healing. It really is about deepening the understanding of our "Broken Treasures and Lost Dreams."

Chapter Two

If God Loves Me Then Why…?

To say, "God loves me unconditionally", is more often than not, a euphemism in the minds of many people. At a heartfelt level, it is a concept that is difficult to connect with. In talking with many African Americans about God's unconditional love, the following responses are pretty typical:

> *I know that God loves me unconditionally. I do not question that at all. However, I have difficulty receiving that love. I have never been loved unconditionally by anyone, and I don't know how it feels to be loved unconditionally. I truly love my children unconditionally so I am able to give that kind of love, but just not receive it. How do I learn to receive unconditional love?* (J. P.)

> *I find this concept of unconditional love a little overwhelming and disconcerting. Since unconditional love is not very likely in this life, it is not something I can completely grasp yet. I know in my head that God loves me. I just have a hard time believing it with my heart. There are just too many things that happen that I have no control over for me to even connect with that idea. For instance,*

why does one group of people have so much, and another has so little, but God is supposed to love us all the same. I love God, and know that a walk with God is an ever growing thing but I am not there yet. Maybe as I get older. (C. M.)

Many African Americans have turned away from Christianity, citing their belief that Christianity not only supported the institution of slavery, but that much of the pain that they experience in the present is at the hand of, would – be – identified – as, evangelical Christians. My heart aches for those who, having had such painful experiences, have yet to reconcile this injury as an act of self-centered, self-willed individuals who are, in fact, themselves, broken.

There are scriptures in the Bible that can be interpreted to frown upon slavery. But there are just as many scriptures that can be interpreted in support of slavery. And to this day there are still those who would attempt to make the Bible simply a moral code, philosophies to appease the wills of men, rather than to see it for what it is, the revelation of God speaking to the hearts of men and women, yet speaking, of the incredible love that He so wants to lavish on His creation. The problem with interpretation is the intent and motivation of the interpreter. And for those individuals who have used the Bible to injure and hold African Americans in abeyance – hanging in the out there somewhere, not fully embraceable as the rest of God's creation, you have equally harmed yourselves.

The question that I would ask is this. If you subscribe to the concept that slavery was an acceptable class of citizenry, as a normal part of life in the Bible then what will you do with the Paul's encounter with Onesimus?

Paul writes an interesting letter to his friend Philemon. The Book of Philemon is a very short Pauline letter. However, at-any-rate, Philemon is a wealthy Christian slave-owner. His slave, Onesimus has run away. Paul encounters Onesimus in his journey and recognizes him as the slave of Philemon. After meeting Paul, Onesimus becomes a Christian – he is converted. Paul sends Onesimus back to Philemon, but he sends him with a letter that contains two powerful points that cannot be dismissed. He writes:

> "Therefore, although in Christ I could be bold and order you to do what you ought to do, yet I appeal to you on the basis of love." [vs.8]

> "Perhaps the reason he was separated from you for a little while was that you might have him back for good - no longer as a slave, but better than a slave, as a dear brother. He is very dear to me but even dearer to you, both as a man and as a brother in the Lord." [vs.16]

Here is a perfect demonstration of the Bible's position, especially the New Testament. Because of Paul's apostolic authority over him, Paul could have forced Philemon to treat Onesimus as a man equal in every way, rather than as a slave. Paul chose to challenge Philemon, instead, appealing to the unconditional law of love upon which the gospel is centered. In effect Paul was saying, this is your brother and to treat him in anyway less than as a brother is uncharitable and violates all that the Kingdom of God stands for.

God's love is unconditional. It is a love that invites us into brotherhood and unity. Christian transformation flows out of this kind of love. But for many African Americans, it is difficult to know this unconditional love because it has never been known in any human relationship.

I am keenly aware that there are, in all reality and for just cause, African Americans who have a difficult time with the concept of God as a loving, benevolent father who cares for his children, who means them well and who will vindicate them for the ills perpetrated upon them by their detractors. The duplicity of such theologizing, as many will argue, rests within the framework of two crucial elements: God as Father, and God as loving. If the operative scenario is one embellished in benevolence and goodwill, there is little to substantiate the caring or good characteristics of God, as father from a practical perspective. Many African Americans have not experienced God in this way.

The framework or reference point for how we understand God's love begins with our experience of mom and dad. This is largely true, but for African Americans it is much deeper than how we experienced mom and dad. It is also steeped in our experience of godly systems and institutions that hold themselves out as honorable and helpful. And, it is also rooted in society's view of us as being worthy of God's love and goodness. Let me explain.

The political and systemic adversaries that have loomed over African American life are difficult barriers to overcome. For the sake of understanding, consider policy innovations relative to families in the 1960s. A rule primarily aimed at African American households, considered a home unsuitable and immoral if there was a man living in that house who was not married to the mother, even if he was the father of the children of that household. The "Man-in-the-House Rule" allowed states to deny eligibility for income assistance through the AFDC program on the grounds that a home was "unsuitable" because the woman's children were illegitimate.

This infamous "Man-in-the-House Rule", stated a child who otherwise qualified for welfare benefits was denied those benefits if the child's mother was living with, or having relations with, any single or married able-bodied male. The man was considered a substitute father, even if the man was not supporting the child. This ruling was a significant feature of the

"War on Poverty." The fall out of this policy would mean that the number of unmarried couples living together in the United States would be ten times larger today than in 1970. That also meant that many of these couples would have, and continue to have children that would be raised in unstable homes. It also meant that the rate of dissolution of these non-marriage relationships would be many times higher than that of married couples. And, it meant that female-headed households with children, especially in the African American community, would increase by more than 250 percent since 1970.[13]

During this same time period there was gross disparity in unemployment amongst blacks and whites. Particularly this was true as an incredible number of African American Men could not find employment. By 1960 the unemployment rate was 2:1 and exceeded this level by 1990. It was the persistence of high black unemployment rates that was largely blamed for "exacerbating the social dislocations associated with urban poverty".[14]

It is not coincidental in any respect that it was during this period of time that African American father absenteeism began to escalate. The feeling being that as a black man, "my children can be cared for better if I am not in the house". And with the pressing

---

[13] Man-in-the-House Rule. 2005. West's Encyclopedia of American Law

[14] Wilson, W. J. 1987. *The Declining Significance of Race*. Chicago: University Press

unemployment issue, the only way that many African American families could survive was if there was no "Man-in-the-House". So systemically, it is difficult for African Americans to connect with God's paternal benevolence, when the very world that we live in engages in subversive patricide, where those who are in power, by their policies and practices co-opt hope leading to a death like disbelief that God is for us.

Life Application

There is a gross disparity between what the Bible teaches as the religion of Jesus, and the way it has been lived out in mainstream, conservative America. In large measure there still is a "we – them" mentality in conservative American religion. That is the religion that preaches that there is master and slave, oppressor and oppressed. It is that kind of thinking about the God of love that allows governments to enact such policies as "Man in the House" and that empowers the oppressor while relegating the oppressed to a compromised and unsuccessful life.

When Christians teach that one group is less worthy than another group – using scripture to support such beliefs, they cannot see the disconnect between the Jesus of the Bible and the way they have treated African Americans. The sadness is that so much of society's response to African Americans in general is out of this mind set – even in the 21st century.

As a young man I recall a conversation with a "saintly" older white gentleman. I asked him to help me understand the scripture "slave obey your master" in light of the scripture that says "there is neither slave nor free". I recall his answer… "in order for slaves to go heaven they must be obedient to their earthly masters and not be discontent with their position in life". He went on to say that this refers to the differences in races today. My response was uncharitable so I will move on.

There is either one God who loves all people or there must be a white god and a black god. The God that our fore parents' knew was the God who got angry at injustice. This is the God who saw all of his children as holy and refused to allow pharaoh to keep them captive. That is why he sent Moses to tell pharaoh, "Let my people go."

This is the one God, the true God, whom I believe loves us. His heart is broken over human-kind's inability to connect the dots… "red, and yellow, black and white, all are precious in his sight". This is the God that I believe loves me. Society has done much to obscure this view of God in African American life. There are so many social deficits, injustices, and inequities that we must combat. But we cannot allow that to keep us at a distance. He is an up close and personal God.

A liberationist view of the scriptures demands equity for all of God's children. Jesus demanded as much. "One is not free if one's mind is enslaved, and our minds were enslaved to the idea that we were ugly and inferior. Black liberation theology re-explained to us some things that had been explained to us incorrectly from the moment we began to learn Christianity".[15] The things that have created pain for us – things that have crippled us emotionally, socially, and spiritually have been creatively designed by the evil one, satan, the devil, to make us focus on the "we" and "them" mentality that causes us to war against each other.

It was Mohandas Gandhi, who said if people followed the Gospels, doing what Jesus asked of us, the world would be revolutionized. Susan K. Smith, a Yale Divinity graduate, Pastor of Advent United Church of Christ in Columbus Ohio wrote in the August 30, 2010 edition of the Washington Post...

> *Liberation theology has made it possible for people other than white people, or more specifically, white males, to feel like there is a place for them in the Kingdom. Liberation theology has not only freed African Americans from an oppressive ideology which has been passed off as theology, but has freed white women as well.*

---

[15] Susan K. Smith. September 2008, On Faith, The Washington Post

> And liberation theology teaches that those who know Jesus will do what Jesus commands: love one another and forgive one another. Liberation theology teaches that if we do not forgive those who have wronged us, we cannot hope to be forgiven.[16]

There are too many African Americans who do not like themselves. For that reason alone I appreciate "Liberation Theology" as an understanding of the God who was and is on the side of the oppressed. Black Liberation theology has succeeded in freeing African Americans from the grip of the negative opinions of those who do not know us.

In this country, where the master-slave, oppressor-oppressed relationships have existed and have been protected on every level – social, economic, and political, there is much to be forgiven. This is the starting place if we are to really experience the God of love in all its fullness.

Not only must we look at mom, dad, me, and the inverse impact of those relationships, but we must also look at we, them, and me; "we", meaning the larger African American community, "them", meaning the overarching systems, society and government, and "me", as the individual thusly impacted by these inverse relationships as well.

---

[16] Smith, Susan k. August 30, 2010. On Faith, The Washington Post

Chapter Three

It's So Hard For Me To Trust

Trust is a crucial issue in African American life. Trust between individuals can be viewed as a form of "social capital" meaning that it is the product of relationships where fellow citizens work with each other, rather than against each other. Defining trust as a moral value that we learn early life, it is the belief that we have goodwill towards others and others also have goodwill towards us. Trust allows us to believe that the world is a good place – that the world is filled with good people, and that these good people have our wellbeing at heart. But trust is not always about the violations of one person against another. At least it is larger than that in the African American community. Here, trust also has to do with institutions and systems at large – how they affect the wellbeing of African Americans.

In his work, *Trust and Social Bonds*, Uslaner states, "At the aggregate level, the roots of trust rest most clearly on economic equality: Across time and states in the United States and across nations (without a legacy of communism), economic equality is the strongest determinant of trust."[17] I believe this is the primary juncture of "mistrust" and "distrust" in the African American community.

The relatively gross disparity in economic status and opportunities experienced by blacks in this country is an inarguable contention. The 'haves' versus the 'have not's' is observable in nearly every dimension of the social strata. The general suspicion of many African Americans is that those who are in power (the haves) intentionally and with great effort work to keep those who are not in power (the have not's) from an equitable access to wealth and economic opportunities and resources.

In the instances where some African Americans have managed, to some degree, to acquire wealth, it has fostered a form of reflexive racism in which blacks who have are suspicious of and in some instances disdain, blacks who have not. This creates trust barriers within the group based on a similar have versus have not dynamic.

Trust issues within the African American community are not limited to economics. Overall, African Americans have poorer health than white Americans. There is 'distrust' in the degree to which African Americans believe that they can have fair and equitable medical access or treatment. In the February 2009 issue of Archives of Pediatric and

---

[17] Uslaner, Eric, *Trust and Social Bonds.* Political Research Quarterly, September, 2004, Vol. 57 No. 3, 501-507

Adolescent Medicine it was reported that black parents are more likely to distrust medical research than white parents.[18] As a result, among minority groups African Americans are frequently under-represented in clinical research. The study cited poverty, lack of awareness, access to medical care, transportation and individual attitudes may contribute to this reluctance.

The goal of this study was to evaluate and compare the attitudes and trust expressed by black and white parents about having their children participate in medical research. The study concluded that the degree of parental distrust toward medical research was significantly greater among African Americans, even after controlling for education. In short, African American parents were more likely to believe that medical research involved too much risk to the participant and that physicians will not make full disclosures regarding their child's participation.

The genesis of such distrust is deep-rooted in a number of such occurrences that can be recalled in the African American experience. Probably, the most renown, with the most devastating and far reaching impact on trust, as it relates to African American confidence in social structures, and systems is the Tuskegee Syphilis Experiment.

---

[18] 2009, Archives of Pediatric and Adolescent Medicine, *http://archpedi.ama-assn.org, accessed September 6, 2010*

The Tuskegee Syphilis Experiment

Bad Blood: The Tuskegee Syphilis Experiment,
James H. Jones, (New York: Free Press, 1993)

For forty years between 1932 and 1972, the U.S. Public Health Service (PHS) conducted an experiment on 399 black men in the late stages of syphilis. These men, for the most part illiterate sharecroppers from one of the poorest counties in Alabama, were never told what disease they were suffering from or of its seriousness. Informed that they were being treated for "bad blood," their doctors had no intention of curing them of syphilis at all. The data for the experiment was to be collected from autopsies of the men, and they were thus deliberately left to degenerate under the ravages of tertiary syphilis—which can include tumors, heart disease, paralysis, blindness, insanity, and death. "As I see it," one of the doctors involved explained, "we have no further interest in these patients until they die."

Using Human Beings as Laboratory Animals

The true nature of the experiment had to be kept from the subjects to ensure their cooperation. The sharecroppers' grossly disadvantaged lot in life made them easy to manipulate. Pleased at the prospect of free medical care – almost none of them had ever seen a doctor before – these unsophisticated and trusting men became the pawns in what James Jones, author of the excellent history on the subject, *"Bad Blood",* identified as "the longest non-therapeutic experiment on human beings in medical history."

The study was meant to discover how syphilis affected blacks as opposed to whites—the theory being that whites experienced more neurological complications from syphilis whereas blacks were more susceptible to cardiovascular damage. How this knowledge would have changed clinical treatment of syphilis is uncertain. Although the PHS touted the study as one of great scientific merit, from the outset its actual benefits were hazy. It took almost forty years before someone involved in the study took a hard and honest look at the end results, reporting that "nothing learned will prevent, find, or cure a single case of infectious syphilis or bring us closer to our basic mission of controlling venereal disease in the United States." When the experiment was brought to the attention of the media in 1972, news anchor Harry Reasoner described it as an experiment that "used human beings as laboratory animals in a long and inefficient study of how long it takes syphilis to kill someone."

A Heavy Price in the Name of Bad Science

By the end of the experiment, 28 of the men had died directly of syphilis, 100 were dead of related complications, 40 of their wives had been infected, and 19 of their children had been born with congenital syphilis. How had these men been induced to endure a fatal disease in the name of science? To persuade the community to support the experiment, one of the original doctors admitted it "was necessary to carry on this study under the guise of a demonstration and provide treatment." At first, the men were prescribed the syphilis remedies of the day—bismuth, neoarsphenamine, and mercury—but in such small amounts that only 3 percent showed any improvement. These token doses of medicine were good public relations and did not interfere with the true aims of the study. Eventually, all syphilis treatment was replaced with "pink medicine"—aspirin. To ensure that the men would show up for a painful and potentially dangerous spinal tap, the PHS doctors misled them with a letter full of promotional hype: "Last Chance for Special Free Treatment." The fact that autopsies would eventually be required was also concealed. As a doctor explained, "If the colored population becomes aware that accepting free hospital care means a post-mortem, every darky will leave Macon County..." Even the Surgeon General of the United States participated in enticing the men to remain in the experiment, sending them certificates of appreciation after 25 years in the study.

Following Doctors' Orders

It takes little imagination to ascribe racist attitudes to the white government officials who ran the experiment, but what can one make of the numerous African Americans who collaborated with them? The experiment's name comes from the Tuskegee Institute, the black university founded by Booker T.

Washington. Its affiliated hospital lent the PHS its medical facilities for the study, and other predominantly black institutions as well as local black doctors also participated. A black nurse, Eunice Rivers, was a central figure in the experiment for most of its forty years. The promise of recognition by a prestigious government agency may have obscured the troubling aspects of the study for some. A Tuskegee doctor, for example, praised "the educational advantages offered our interns and nurses as well as the added standing it will give the hospital." Nurse Rivers explained her role as one of passive obedience: "we were taught that we never diagnosed, we never prescribed; we followed the doctor's instructions!" It is clear that the men in the experiment trusted her and that she sincerely cared about their well-being, but her unquestioning submission to authority eclipsed her moral judgment. Even after the experiment was exposed to public scrutiny, she genuinely felt nothing ethical had been amiss.

One of the most chilling aspects of the experiment was how zealously the *PHS* kept these men from receiving treatment. When several nationwide campaigns to eradicate venereal disease came to Macon County, the men were prevented from participating. Even when penicillin was discovered in the 1940s—the first real cure for syphilis—the Tuskegee men were deliberately denied the medication. During World War II, 250 of the men registered for the draft and were consequently ordered to get treatment for syphilis, only to have the

PHS exempt them. Pleased at their success, the PHS representative announced: "So far, we are keeping the known positive patients from getting treatment." The experiment continued in spite of the Henderson Act (1943), a public health law requiring testing and treatment for venereal disease, and in spite of the World Health Organization's Declaration of Helsinki (1964), which specified that "informed consent" was needed for experiment involving human beings.

Blowing the Whistle

The story finally broke in the *Washington Star* on July 25, 1972, in an article by Jean Heller of the Associated Press. Her source was Peter Buxtun, a former PHS venereal disease interviewer and one of the few whistle blowers over the years. The PHS, however, remained unrepentant, claiming the men had been "volunteers" and "were always happy to see the doctors," and an Alabama state health officer who had been involved claimed "somebody is trying to make a mountain out of a molehill."

Under the glare of publicity, the government ended their experiment, and for the first time provided the men with effective medical treatment for syphilis. Fred Gray, a lawyer who had previously defended Rosa Parks and Martin Luther King, filed a class action suit that provided a $10 million out-of-court settlement for the men and their families. Gray, however, named only whites and white organizations in the suit, portraying Tuskegee as a black and white case when it was in fact more complex than that—

black doctors and institutions had been involved from beginning to end.

The PHS did not accept the media's comparison of Tuskegee with the appalling experiments performed by Nazi doctors on their Jewish victims during World War II. Yet in addition to the medical and racist parallels, the PHS offered the same morally bankrupt defense offered at the Nuremberg trials: they claimed they were just carrying out orders, mere cogs in the wheel of the PHS bureaucracy, exempt from personal responsibility.

The study's other justification—for the greater good of science—is equally spurious. Scientific protocol had been shoddy from the start. Since the men had in fact received some medication for syphilis in the beginning of the study, however inadequate, it thereby corrupted the outcome of a study of "untreated syphilis."

In 1990, a survey found that 10 percent of African Americans believed that the U.S. government created AIDS as a plot to exterminate blacks, and another 20 percent could not rule out the possibility that this might be true. As preposterous and paranoid as this may sound, at one time the Tuskegee experiment must have seemed equally farfetched. Who could imagine the government, all the way up to the Surgeon General of the United States, deliberately allowing a group of its citizens to die from a terrible disease for the sake of an ill-conceived experiment? In light of this and many other shameful episodes in our history, African Americans' widespread mistrust of the government and white society in general should not be a surprise to anyone.

May 16, 1997, Then President William (Bill) Clinton apologized to the eight remaining survivors of this atrocity denouncing it as a clearly racist activity. " The United States government did something that was wrong—deeply, profoundly, morally wrong. It was an outrage to our commitment to integrity and equality for all our citizens. . . . clearly racist."

Life Application

Trust issues in the African American community are deep. Whether it is about health care, equitable housing, education, the judicial process, or economics, of the issues that have the most far reaching effect on African American life, racism is at the center of the feelings of mistrust. In fact, this is true as it relates to how African Americans are perceived in culture altogether. Of the three main minorities in this country, Blacks, Hispanics, and Asians, there is very little trust for each other. In a New American Media (NAM) poll December 12, 2007, [19] "this extraordinary poll reveals some unflattering realities that exist in America today," said Sandy

---

[19] New American Media poll December, 12 2007, http://news.newamericamedia.org/news/

Close, head of New America Media which sponsored the poll together with ethnic media groups. The poll's findings:

> *Forty-four percent of Hispanics and 47 percent of Asians are "afraid of African-Americans because they are responsible for most of the crime," the survey of 1,105 adults drawn from the three ethnic groups showed.*
>
> *More than half of black Americans polled and 46 percent of Hispanics said Asian business owners do not treat them with respect.*
>
> *And half of African-Americans said Latin American immigrants "are taking jobs, housing and political power away from the black community."*
>
> *Hispanics and Asians, whose populations are made up mainly of immigrants, were positive about the American dream, saying that those who work hard in the United States reap the rewards of their toil.*
>
> *In contrast, more than 60 percent of African-Americans dismissed the American dream as not working for them.*
>
> *All three ethnic groups viewed white Americans in a more favorable light than they did members of another minority.*
>
> *Sixty-one percent of Hispanics, 54 percent of Asians and 47 percent of African-Americans said*

they would rather do business with whites than members of the other two groups.

With such prevalence of prejudiced thoughts it is not difficult to determine that the issue of trust will continue to be a prevalent factor in minority life, especially as it relates to African American life. But there is yet another determinant relative to African Americans and trust that cannot be ignored. It touches over 70% of all African American households. It has to do with how racial disparities in incarceration impact African American families.

Hamedah Hasan, a devoted mother of three, fled a physically abusive relationship and sought shelter with her cousin. Hamedah's primary goal was to provide a safe living environment for herself and her three children. After several months of living with her cousin, he began asking her to run minor errands for his drug operation. Although she never used drugs and felt she had no choice but to participate at the time, Hamedah admittedly chose to engage in the wrong doing.

In 1993, she was charged with conspiracy to deliver crack cocaine, which made her liable for all drugs ever associated with her cousin's drug operation, regardless of the role she played. As a result, Hamedah was sentenced to 27 years in prison.

Hamedah's charge was a first time, nonviolent offense. To date she has already served 16 years behind bars. As a result, the federal prison system has paid approximately $410,000 dollars to incarcerate and keep Hamedah locked away. In addition, Hamedah's children have grown up without their mother present in their daily lives.

Hamedah Hasan's story is told here simply because it is an extraordinary exception that suggests the degree to which society tends towards the incarceration of African Americans, including African American women. In 2001, the chances of going to prison for an African American female (5.6%) was proportionately the same as for white males (5.9%). The life-time chances of going to prison for white females was 0.9% and Hispanic females (2.2%). The highest chances of incarceration is among black males (32.2%), followed by Hispanic males (17.2%) and again, lowest among white males (5.9%).[20]

What is most disturbing about these statistics is that they represent a pain-filled reality in African American families. Today, over *500,000* African American fathers are currently incarcerated in America's prisons. Even more striking is the impact incarceration has on high school dropouts. According

---

[20] Sabol, William J., PhD, and Couture, Heather, Bureau of Justice Statistics, Prison Inmates at Midyear 2007 (Washington, DC: US Department of Justice, June 2008), NCJ221944, p. 7.

to the report, more young (*20* to 34-year-old) African American men without a high school diploma are currently behind bars (*37 percent*) than employed (*26 percent*) in American society today. As high school drop outs become more of a problem in American schools, this statistic should cause all of us great concern now and for the future.

It is significant to note, Human Rights Watch's analysis of prison admission data for 2003 revealed that relative to population, blacks are 10.1 times more likely than whites to be sent to prison for drug offenses.

> The racial disparities in the rates of drug arrests culminate in dramatic racial disproportions among incarcerated drug offenders. At least two-thirds of drug arrests result in a criminal conviction. Many convicted drug offenders are sentenced to incarceration: an estimated 67 percent of convicted felony drug defendants are sentenced to jail or prison. The likelihood of incarceration increases if the defendant has a prior conviction. Since blacks are more likely to be arrested than whites on drug charges, they are more likely to acquire the convictions that ultimately lead to higher rates of incarceration. Although the data in this backgrounder indicate that blacks represent about one-third of drug arrests, they constitute 46 percent of persons convicted of drug felonies in state courts. Among black defendants convicted of drug offenses, 71 percent received sentences to incarceration in contrast

to 63 percent of convicted white drug offenders.[21]

Additionally, African American men make up 62.7 percent of all drug offenders admitted to state prisons. White males make up 36.7 percent of all drug offenders admitted to state prisons. While federal surveys and other data show clearly that this racial disparity bears scant relation to racial differences in drug offending, there are, five times more white drug users than black. Therefore, relative to population, black men are admitted to state prison on drug charges at a rate that is 13.4 times greater than that of white men. In large part because of the extraordinary racial disparities in incarceration for drug offenses, blacks are incarcerated for all offenses at 8.2 times the rate of whites. One in every 20 black men over the age of 18 in the United States is in state or federal prison, compared to one in 180 white men.[22]

African-Americans make up about 12 percent of the U.S. population, yet they make up nearly half the prison population. Consequently, the issues around racial profiling, prejudice, and the mass incarceration of African Americans is a justice issue that make it increasingly more difficult for African

---

[21] Fellner, Jamie, "Decades of Disparity: Drug Arrests and Race in the United States," Human Rights Watch (New York, NY: March 2009), p. 16

[22] Human Rights Watch, "Racial Disparities in the War on Drugs" (Washington, DC: Human Rights Watch, 2000). http://www.hrw.org/legacy/reports/2000/usa/Rcedrg00-01.htm#P149_24292

Americans to trust. The statistical data alone suggests that the legal and judicial system in this country supports the overall attitude of prejudice and suspicion towards blacks. In 2001, Jesse Jackson charged,

> *Our states now spend more on prisons than on universities. We are increasingly becoming a nation of first-class jails and second-class schools. Most rural and urban schools are not wired for the Internet, but nearly all of the jails are. The United States is spending an average of $5,500 per year to educate a youth, and almost $20,000 [four times as much] to lock up a youth.*[23]

Without significant changes, the system will continue to have a devastating impact on African American families, their children and society until something is done about it.

---

[23] Jackson, Jesse. 2001. *Liberty and Justice for All: Mass Incarceration Comes at a Moral Cost to Every American*. The Good Shepherd Restoration Ministries.

Chapter Four

Lord, I Hurt

My wound is severe, and my grief is great.
My sickness is incurable, but I must bear it.
Jeremiah 10:19 (NLT)

Pain is not an unfamiliar emotion to God. The prophet, Jeremiah, in describing his pain and the pain of the people of Israel, suggests the depths of despair to which hurting people surrender; "my wound is severe" – "my grief is great". Identifying evil upon evil, atrocity upon atrocity, the weeping prophet is heart sick because the people will not listen to his call to repentance. They relish in the declarations of priest and prophets who "have treated the wound of my people carelessly saying, 'peace, peace,' when there is no peace" (Jeremiah 8:11). Denouncing the perversity of the whole nation, he grieves for the wounded. He mourns for the broken of Israel. In Jeremiah 8:18 – 9: 1, we read,

> *My joy is gone, grief is upon me, my heart is sick. Hark, the cry of my poor people from far and wide in the land: "Is the LORD not in Zion? Is her King not in her?" ("Why have they provoked me to anger with their images, with their foreign idols?")*

"The harvest is past, the summer is ended, and we are not saved." For the hurt of my poor people I am hurt, I mourn, and dismay has taken hold of me. Is there no balm in Gilead? Is there no physician there? Why then has the health of my poor people not been restored? O that my head were a spring of water, and my eyes a fountain of tears, so that I might weep day and night for the slain of my poor people!

The "Jeremiad", a term ascribed to the lamentations of Jeremiah, is synonymous with the pain of many African Americans. This term, so coined describes an outlook on life that is filled with pessimism and no hope in the future. It is a sense and feeling that things will not, and cannot get better. Jeremiah's heart is poured out because of the hurt and despair of the people. He cries at the destruction of Jerusalem, largely at the hands of willful priests and prophets who, disobeying God, are only concerned about their own health and welfare – ignoring the plight of the poor and marginalized.

It is this same sense of forlorn and abandonment that many African Americans have experienced. And out of their experience the jeremiad questions are echoed: "Is the Lord not in Zion?" "Is there no balm in Gilead?" – "Is there no physician there?" And, as the pain of the Jeremiah tradition was passed down from community of faith to community of faith through the years, so it has been with African Americans. As these passages speaks of the prophet's longing to see God work within the historical places of pain and brokenness in the lives of Israel, an eschatological hope of similar proportions is birthed in the hearts of contemporary African American life. In this culture, living in the shadows of similar pain, there is a longing for the Great Physician - God. He has promised to heal, to deliver, and to redeem.

The complexities of life, for many African American peoples, are heightened and escalate into compounded issues rooted in a history of maltreatment. The memories of discrimination, marginalization, name calling, berating, and segregation colors the landscape of life. Hope is obscure. Dreams are deferred. Sometimes the pain runs so deep – protracted, multilayered pain, that the victim is anesthetized by the pain itself. Life, riddled with these many complexities becomes normative, creating and prescribing the standard by which one expects to live by.

The issues that are faced, within the community, becomes the same for everyone in the community. No one is exempt. No matter how smart, sophisticated, or savvy; whether you are creative, courageous, or complacent, the common denominator is this shared reality of pain. It is a pain that is so pervasive that no one in the community is unaffected. It is pain not only unique to black people, but uniquely experienced by black people – sons and daughters of the Diaspora – African Americans assimilated into a westernized cultural context. Racism, insidious, engrained, deliberately infecting every corner of life. This reality impacts one's spiritual development, one's perspective on self, family and every human relationship. And as complex are the issues that gather around African American life, equally complex are the coping mechanisms for managing the trauma and fallout.

The resilience of African Americans in the face of all that has been experienced is amazing. As a historically resilient people, faith and a strong belief in the "God of our fathers", has been the most sustaining dynamic for the healing of emotional pain. In the face of every trauma, of every disastrous and debilitating circumstance of life, faith has been respite care and survival skill. While many African Americans have a deep spirituality and belief in God, many are no longer involved in church. The reasons for this lack of involvement are many and varied. But the common thread of thought is that in the church, faith is confronted. The testing of one's faith collides with one's belief creating a crisis in faith's ability to trust God – to wait on him to deliver.

Faith has been the key for overcoming the traumatic experiences of a past that is equally present and for dealing with racism that is also past, yet present. And, when faith has failed to produce the essential anesthesia for coping with the traumas of life it has given way to anger. This anger is largely related to the inability to reconcile the blessed hope to one's experienced reality. Anger has its own fallout. Equally effective in killing pain, but far more deadly in that it is most often internally directed first – destroying the fabric of faith, eroding hope, and creating a dynamic of suspicion, mistrust, and existential despair.

Jeremiah's grief is a reflection of God's grief. In Terrence Fretheim's, *The Suffering of God,* we are helped to understand "grief" and "suffering" as appropriate to describe God's feelings about our brokenness. God does not take delight in our pain. But God is grieved, and God does hurt, because of the sins of his people, and the consequences of those sins.[24]

In shifting the focus to look at where we begin to find healing for systemic pain, we must start by honoring the reality – "this pain is real". To deny the message stemming from this pain is to deny, to dishonor, and to violate the experience of the sufferer. For it is within the framework of understanding the experiences, affirming them as true and real, that one is able to begin moving towards an understanding of where God is at work in the rhythms and dynamics of one's life.

In a real sense, the anger that is felt and often expressed is a disappointment in one's ability to love

---

[24] Fretheim, Terrence. 2006. *The Suffering of God an Old Testament Perspective.* Minneapolis: Fortress

and hold tenaciously to faith in the God of love. Because, love and faith have failed to produce the fulfillment of the blessed hope, disappointment gives way to anger and bargaining. After all, anger and bargaining – these are stages of grief. Grief is the story of losses. Grief is the story of losses filled with sorrow and heartache, difficult to process and resolve – the source of many deep woundings, often carried at the surface of one's experience. As grief works its way outward, its corporate impact on the African American community is sustained by the repeated messages, injuries and experiences that are repeated over and over again that both, deny place, and voice in majority culture.

Life Application

In *Race Matters*, Cornell West suggests "Black people's rage ought to target white supremacy..."[25] White supremacy, for our understanding, is a generalized belief that white people are superior to people of other racial backgrounds. While this thought may be held by some white people, I do not believe it is held by all. As such, I subscribe to the belief that white supremacy is more of a political ideology.

In their 1968 book *Black Rage,* Grier and Cobbs argue that black people, living in a racist, white

---

[25] West, Cornell. 1994. *Race Matters.* New York: Vintage Books

supremacist society, are psychologically damaged by the effects of racist oppression. Further, they argue, because of the damage caused by racism, in certain situations, black people act in ways that appear to be 'abnormal' to majority culture. Pondering on this thought a litany of such situations, in which responses may seem abnormal come to mind. One example is the difference in a black person's response to law officials, and that of a white person's. When a white person is walking the streets and sees a policeman or law official, in most instances that individual feels a sense of peace, protection and safety. Conversely, when a black person is walking the streets and sees a policeman or law official, in most instances that individual will feel threatened, fearful and anxious - especially if it is a black male!

Grier and Cobbs sites numerous examples of similar scenarios, "To live near blacks or to eat with blacks is to jeopardize one's status. White people are supposed to eat and live in better places than black people".[26] This statement is followed by a discussion that illustrates the central attitude of white superiority that still holds true in many instances.

> *The value of a home has come to be determined neither by the quality of the structure nor by the value of the structures around it. It can be sharply devalued by the proximity of a family of blacks... We know of no other ethnic group which by its*

---

[26] Cobbs, Price and Grier, Williams. 1968. *Black Rage, p. 158.* New York: Basic Books

> *mere proximity can so certainly make a man's home repugnant to him.* [27]

Then, there is the story of the white girl who told her mother she was engaged to a 'Negro' – the mother fainted. Upon recovery, she asked her daughter: "What color is he – light or dark?" Next she asked: "Does he have any money?" And finally: "What does he do?" It is difficult enough for an African American to enjoy place and welcome in culture. Even in the present day, there are some misgivings about 'mixed' relationships all of which are rooted in racist attitudes that ascribe value to blacks in an almost ranking fashion. It works like this: if he or she is fair skinned, or very rich, or have some powerful position in society, it in some way neutralizes the fact of being black. And, there are many such occurrences and experiences as these within the African American community; painful, hurtful, experiences – dubbed as usual. Such are the foundational layers of unacknowledged and often generalized pain – echoed in Baldwin's *Notes of a Native Son*, "I have not written about being a Negro at such length because I do not expect that to be my only subject, but only because it was the gate I had to unlock before I could hope to write about anything else."[28]

I began this chapter with a simple proposition – pain is not an unfamiliar emotion to God, and, it is not.

---

[27] Ibid, p. 158
[28] Baldwin, James. 1961. *Notes of a Native Son.* New York: Double Day

Nonetheless, there are many hurting people. I have a burden for the pain of black people, especially the unacknowledged, unaddressed sources of pain which are both commonplace and often minimized as normal. That is precisely what has happened in the lives of many individuals whom I encounter day after day. They have normalized their pain and have settled for less than the wholeness that God promises. There is a balm in Gilead, the Great Physician is here. And he wants to help you dismantle all of the structures and beliefs that you have held to. He wants to meet you in your places of pain and journey with you to a place of healing and wholeness. That is his promise. *"Hear my cry, O God; attend unto my prayer. From the end of the earth will I cry unto thee, when my heart is overwhelmed: lead me to the rock that is higher than I" (Psalm 61:1, 2).*

Chapter Five

Who Told You That?

"O God, from my youth you have taught me, and I still proclaim your wondrous deeds. So even to old age and gray hairs, O God, do not forsake me, until I proclaim your might to all the generations to come. Your power and your righteousness, O God, reach the high heavens."
Psalm 71:17-18

Many African Americans have worked hard to overcome the ill effects of slavery, and the resultant attitude held by many that African Americans cannot achieve or be successful beyond sports or athletics. However, with a firm conviction of God's justice instilled within them, our forefathers and mothers toiled, giving all that they had to create opportunities that would level the playing field. The fruit of their labor gave birth to what has been identified as, the "Black Middle Class".

Laboring under the belief that achieving middle class status through hard work and education leads to a lifestyle of success and acceptance, it was believed that the adversarial effects of racism could be either escaped or overcome. However, for white America, race continued to blur class distinctions among blacks, meaning that "color" or "race" remained the predominant qualifier for success and acceptance.

Therefore, the black middle class is just another dimension of African American life caught in the vise-grip of racial disparity. Notwithstanding, in African American life and culture, many continue to hold to the idea that if one works hard enough one can achieve "The American Dream". And, there are many, including many African Americans, who suggest that blacks have not achieved because they have not worked hard enough. There are others who believe that programs like "Affirmative Action" create a 'give – it – to – me – I – don't – have – to – work – for – it' mentality among some blacks. Embracing this belief they will cite the fact that other ethnic minorities come into this country and "get their piece" of the American dream – why can't blacks?

Those who hold to this position overlook two significant truths:

1. As African Americans, black people did not come to this country voluntarily. They arrived in chains and were brought here through trickery and deceit as inferior persons – as chattel.

Even after emancipation blacks have struggled with acceptance of each other and acceptance by the larger society. Equal opportunity has been elusive in many arenas of life simply because of the country's struggle to accord equality and parity to a people that the country once enslaved. This seems to be the primary resistance to embracing African Americans fully. No other group arrived to these shores in chains.

> 2. Immigrant groups arrive to these shores, in many respects with either, education and a belief in the American Dream, or with substantial internal support and resources that makes the American Dream attainable for them.

Undeniably, there is a "black middle class". These are black people who have made it in America despite the odds, believing in the work ethic of their fathers. These are skilled and educated individuals with strong family backgrounds, where emphasis has been placed on success and achievement. But in defining themselves as such, the standard is that mirrored by what is seen as success in mainstream culture. And there is a tendency for those blacks who "have made it" to look at those who "have not made it" as lower class in similar fashion as the 'house slave vs. field slave mentality. In the 60's this 'bourgeoisie' designation created an identity disparity within the black culture that fostered class tensions within the race.

This tension became another source of black pain that was, in many instances, not dealt with. Those who considered themselves middle class dissociated from those who were not. Successful blacks often subjected fellow blacks to similar character indictments and criticisms as whites. The fact is that there were still many blacks without skills who suffered from educational and social deficiencies that perpetuated poverty and embellished the idea of "lower class". Some were even homeless. Some were in hopeless situations. Some were seduced by the 'quick' money of drugs and crime. Some were not able to negotiate the educational, academic and economic maize that could assure them that they could arrive to the shores of the black middle class. But this one fact remained, all were still black. These were and are our sisters and brothers. And when the larger dominant culture looks at us, they do not see us in our varying stages of achievement or lack thereof. They see us as black.

The implied separatism is hurting us. For all intents and purposes, for us, class and race is synonymous. Because our very presence is rooted in a shared history of pain, our collective efforts should be aimed at healing our pain. It is counterproductive to give support to the dysfunctional behaviors that are prevalent within our communities. But we can produce a positive result when our attention is turned to the would – be victimizer; the would – be violator; the would – be abuser; the would – be substance user. Our community is hurting and continues to suffer as long as we do not fully embrace who we are as a collective people and approach our corporate brokenness from a place of deep caring and longing for the healing of the community as a whole.

Who told you that you are inferior or less than? Who told you that you cannot achieve and be all that you could ever dream of being? Who told you that? These are rhetorical questions that find their answers in all of the underlying beliefs that we have embraced about ourselves from people and systems that have difficulty affirming our value. But we, together can work towards the wholeness that we, as a community deserve and are desperate for.

It begins with what we tell ourselves. To be whole is to be entire and without lack. Wholeness begins, for us, with affirming the truth… "for I am fearfully and wonderfully made, and that my soul knows right well" (Psalm 139:14).

For many of us, life has been difficult. There are those rare gems of the black community that have enjoyed privilege, success, and some measure of acclaim. That must not be a reason to perpetuate a separatist and divisive stratagem that creates a war within the community between the "haves" and the "have-nots". We all live in the same community even though there may be physical, geographical distances between us. When we see ourselves as separatist, as one who has versus one who has not, we engage in a form of corporate dysfunctional behavior that reinforces our common pain.

Those, in our community, who have enjoyed such favor must look on the rest of us and discover that we are all gems – of infinite worth and value. To regard each other's preciousness is to defeat the strategies of culture that are designed to keep us unhealthy, broken, and living a life of compromise, defeat and poverty in all of its forms – poor in resources, poor in compassion, poor in connecting, and poor in caring for one another. It is this kind of poverty that inevitably defines blackness and victimization synonymously.

Life Application

Author Shelby Steele, explores the intersection of race and class in the lives of middle-class African Americans. Speaking on the idea of class division within the African American culture he writes:

> *Since it was our victimization more than any other variable that identified and unified us, moreover, it followed logically that the purest black was the poor black. It was images of him that clustered around the positive pole of the race polarity; all other blacks were, in effect, required to identify with him in order to confirm their own blackness.*[29]

He continues…

> *The single story that sat atop the pinnacle of racial victimization for us was that of Emmett Till, the Northern black teen-ager who, on a*

---

[29] Steele, Shelby. 1990. *The content of our character*. New York: Harper Collins.

visit to the South in 1955, was killed and grotesquely mutilated for supposedly looking at or whistling at (we were never sure which, though we argued the point endlessly) a white woman. Oh, how we probed his story, finding in his youth and Northern upbringing the quintessential embodiment of black innocence, brought down by a white evil so portentous and apocalyptic, so gnarled and hideous, that it left us with a feeling not far from awe. By telling his story and others like it, we came to feel the immutability of our victimization, its utter indigenousness, as a thing on this earth like dirt or sand or water.[30]

Similarly, John Jacob, then president and chief executive officer of the National Urban League, before members of Congress in March 1988, addresses the question of how to extend greater opportunities to poor blacks. He begins his speech by briefly citing the goals of the National Urban League as based upon three principles: Advocacy on behalf of black citizens and all poor people; community-based service delivery focusing on job and skills training programs, education, health and housing programs, and a bridge-builder between the races.[31] In Adams' discussion on the progress and advances in equality

---

[30] Ibid
[31] Jacob, John, Steele, S. 1988. *On Being Black and Middle Class*. www.britannica.com/blackhistory/article-9399835

between the races he clearly states there is still a lot of ground to claim.

Like Steele, he concludes that in the eyes of America, regardless of these gains, problems still converge at the place of race. Specifically because,

- Half of all black children grow up in poverty.
- Over a third of all blacks are poor—two million more blacks became poor in the past dozen years.
- Almost two million black workers are jobless—over twelve percent of the black work force, and a rate two-and-a-half times that for whites.
- Black family income is only 58 percent of that of whites; the typical black family earns less than the government itself says is needed for a decent, but modest living standard.
- Black households have less than one-tenth the wealth of white households.
- In this high-tech, information age, black dropout rates in some cities are higher than black graduation rates, and there has been an alarming decline in the numbers of blacks entering college.

In virtually all of those areas, Jacob describes black disadvantage as worse than it has been at any time since the mid-1970s. At the same time he acknowledges the fact that some blacks have made extraordinary progress. We have black judges presiding over court rooms where civil rights demonstrators were once sentenced in the 1950s.

Black executives now help shape policies of corporations that once wouldn't hire blacks. Black professionals live in formerly all-white suburbs and earn middle class incomes. But still, they share with their poorer brothers and sisters a common bond, the bond of blackness. And for that fact, whether affluent or disadvantaged, all blacks suffer from racism.

In 1994, Joe Feagin, a white sociologist, and Melvin Sikes, a black psychologist, conducted interviews and surveyed 209 middle class African Americans. They discovered contrary to the long held belief of many African Americans, blacks do not escape the effects of racism because they have achieved middle class status. They further found that despite the facts that the black middle class is much wealthier, more prestigious, more educated, and growing rapidly, the racist insults of everyday life continue unabated.[32]

Much of the dysfunctional behavior experienced in the lives of many African Americans has to do with wealth or a lack of wealth. This includes feelings generally held about wealth and economic opportunities.

In an August 2010 article, William Reed of *The Business Exchange*, writes about the black middle class describing the past 40 years as the best times ever for Black America. But more recent statistics indicate that the size of the black underclass has tripled since the 1980s. And, the black middle class

---

[32] Feagin, Joe R. and Sikes, Melvin P. 1994.*Living with racism: The black middle class experience*. Boston Mass: Beacon Press

that was thought to be flourishing have fallen on hard times. Studies show: "the wealth gap between white and black American families has more than quadrupled over the last generation."[33]

Robert L. Johnson, founder and chairman of the RJL Companies says "a wealth gap Tsunami threatens African American families". Addressing the Congressional Black Caucus, Johnson advocated legislative activity on the issue saying:

> We must admit the harsh reality of a history of institutionalized racism and economic discrimination against African Americans is the primary cause of wealth disparity between Black and White Americans. Blacks have never caught up economically and according to a 2007 Pew Charitable Trusts study, "nearly half of African Americans born to middle-income parents in the late 1960s plunged into poverty or near-poverty as adults" and "forty-five percent of Black children whose parents were solidly middle class in 1968 – a stratum with a median income of $55,600 in inflation-adjusted dollars – grew up to be among the lowest fifth of the nation's earners, with a median family income of $23,100." The US Census says "White household median net worth is 10 times that of Black households."

---

[33] http://www.theskanner.com/article/As-Black-Middle-Class-Shrinks-Racial-Dialogue-Missing-2010-08-04

African American medium net is $11,800 compared to $118,000 for Whites.[34]

The stark reality is that the disparity in wealth is reflective of societal disparities in general as it relates to African Americans. Researchers of Brandeis University's Institute on Assets and Social Policy say the racial wealth gap "reflects public policies" such as tax cuts on investment income and inheritances which benefit the wealthiest" and "tax deductions for home mortgages, retirement accounts, and college savings all disproportionately benefit higher income families." The study indicates that even assimilated blacks recognize this disparity as an issue of race.[35]

In the more than 160 years after Frederick Douglas said to White America, "The rich inheritance of justice, liberty, prosperity and independence, bequeathed by your fathers, is shared by you, not by me," the masses of African Americans remain at the bottom of the nation's economic ladder. This is one of the major realities of our pain – the fact that too many African Americans continue to suffer from poverty, unemployment, and the inequitable distribution of income and wealth.

Our nation's "establishment" wants Blacks to ignore the racial nexus of wealth disparity between Blacks and Whites. Yet, an even more tender reality is the lack of race-recognition remedies that should be

---

[34] Op. cit.
[35] Research and Policy Brief. May 2010. Institutes of Assets and Social Policy http://iasp.brandeis.edu/pdfs/Racial-Wealth-Gap-Brief.pdf

a part of the healing of our community. We are not "haves" and "have – not's". We are family, intrinsically and uniquely tied together by the bonds of a common history that transcends all of our differences.

Chapter Six

Michael's Story

"I put this in human terms because you are weak in your natural selves. Just as you used to offer the parts of your body in slavery to impurity and to ever-increasing wickedness, so now offer them in slavery to righteousness, leading to holiness. When you were slaves to sin, you were free from the control of righteousness. What benefit did you reap from the things that you are now ashamed of? Those things result in death. But now that you have been set free from sin and have become slaves to God, the benefit you reap leads to holiness, and the result is eternal life. For the wage of sin is death, but the gift of God is eternal life in Christ Jesus our Lord." (Romans 6: 19-23 NIV)

Several years ago I encountered the work of Dr. Terry Wardle, a pioneer in a method of caring called formational counseling. This methodology engages a rubric of care called "The Structures of Healing"

Starting with an examination of one's "Life Situation", the Structures of Healing provides a diagrammatic approach to understanding the source of wounding and the resulting pain within a hurting individual. It demonstrates a way in which you can begin to make sense of your life's experiences while helping you to see where such experiences have inoculated you against acknowledging and honoring your pain. As it relates to your healing, I know of no better approach to peeling back the layers of pain that we have experienced as an African American people. It helps you in unlocking the gate of your false self and allows you to honestly delve into the "stuff" of your life – to unravel the pieces fraught with denial, pretense, frustration and fears. Skillfully employed, this model can initiate you into a more authentic place of living – a place of grace and truth.

STRUCTURES OF HEALING
Dr. Terry Wardle[36]

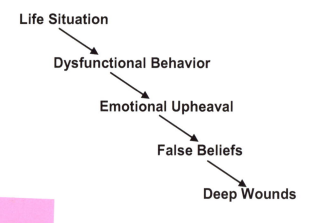

The Structures of Healing is designed to help you see the cause and effect relationship between wounds, false beliefs, emotional upheaval, dysfunctional behavior and your life situation. In examining a

---

[36] Wardle, Terry. 2001. Healing Care Healing Prayer. Siloam Springs, Arkansas: Leafwood Publishers

problem, it begins with the Life Situation. That is because that is what is obvious, what is easily observable. Looking at the rubric you may ask yourself the question, *what is my life situation*?

All of us experience many life situations, but the one that you want to focus on with respect to the Structures of Healing is the one that is compromising your wholeness and wellbeing. It is the situational, circumstantial, or problematic area of your life that is characterized by some level of dysfunction. It is most often a place of protection where you do not allow easy access. But it is from that place the real you lives, acts, and engages others.

An example of a debilitating life situation would be that of an alcoholic, whose life is characterized by excessive drinking. Compromising his wellbeing, his drinking causes problems with his health, in his relationships, and interrupts his abilities to function optimally in the significant areas of his life. Clarifying or understanding what drives the characteristic behavior of the *life situation* – excessive drinking in this case, requires looking at all the landings beneath.

The next landing on this structure is the place of *dysfunction.* Here you ask yourself the question, do I engage in *dysfunctional behaviors* in an effort to meet deep emotional needs in my life – to kill pain? This is a deeply personal question that you want to mine for all that it is worth. This question requires a depth of honesty and truth telling that many individuals never engage, because it is so easy to live in denial.

Any dysfunctional behavior that you engage in is a response to *emotional upheaval*. You probably never thought about it, but there is a reason why you run to the refrigerator for food when you feel upset. For a lot of individuals there is something soothing and comforting about eating when you feel troubled, or drinking for that matter, or even working out at the gym! Every dysfunctional behavior is triggered by some emotional upheaval. Your question – when I experience *emotional upheaval,* am I clear about the source, or do I mask a deeper pain that is rooted in a *wounding* experience that I have normalized, denied, justified or otherwise buried.

Emotional upheaval is closely tied to a prior wounding experience. You may ask, what is a wound? Pain is a part of life. It is also one of the ways we learn to stay safe. However, some pain has an irreparable impact that often affects us emotionally, spiritually, and physically. That kind of pain is wounding in that it alters what we believe about ourselves, the world we live in, others and in many instances it alters what we believe about God. Just as we all have experienced physical wounds, so too we all have experienced emotional wounds. To honor the pain that comes from such wounding is the beginning of emotional health and wellbeing. To ignore the fact that you may have experienced emotional wounding at some point in your life is to hold on to emotions that can diminish your productivity and wholeness.

Continuing on the spectrum, such emotions give rise to *false beliefs* – things we believe to be true about ourselves. Because of our inability to appropriate truth in the places of our pain, like a vicious cycle, present experiences can trigger emotional upheaval that is driven by lies that we believe. These beliefs can stem from many sources. Following the path of the Structures of Healing paradigm, this is the origin or the source of such debilitating beliefs – a wounding experience.

Wounds can occur from things that were said to us, about us that diminished us, berated us or discounted us. Wounds can come from the experiences of things that were perpetrated upon us that we were helpless to defend ourselves against such as abuse, and things that were withheld from us that we needed to thrive, to feel loved, welcomed and safe in the world, such as abandonment.

In our growth and development, many of us had such experiences or received messages about ourselves which were not helpful. These negative messages, rooted in a wounding event, became a part of our core belief structure. Whatever the deficit, or source of wounding, we believed something about ourselves that was not true. We held to this to make sense out of our world, believing ourselves to somehow be responsible. Many of us continue to carry childhood woundings in our present day experiences. Because emotional wounds stem from lies and distorted truths that run deep within our soul, they adversely have an effect on our relationships, and wellbeing usually lodged in such statements as:

- Nothing works out for me
- People are against me.
- People always leave me
- If people really knew me they would have nothing to do with me.
- I am shameful
- I am intrinsically bad
- I deserve whatever I get (punishment)
- Nothing I do is ever good enough
- No one can be trusted.

To compound this, for African Americans, there are systemic wounds that result from our cultural experiences as well. Wounds can come from harsh words, discrimination, loss – especially ungrieved losses, abuse, abandonment, rejection and any number of emotional experiences that demean, or hurt. Specifically in childhood emotional wounds can happen when caretakers abuse their power and act insensitively to the emotional needs of children. For many of us, even as adults, we still feel the pain of harsh words spoken to us at a young age. Not only can such pain last a lifetime, but every new experience and every new relationship, as we grow and go is sifted through the lens of our pain. Wounds are attached to the painful memories still moving within us.

For any healing to occur there has to be a clear connection between the process of healing and that which is being healed. Denial of places of pain and brokenness within a hurting individual actually blocks and can even eliminate the possibility that you can be better. For some individuals, the feelings of resentment, poor performance, lack of acceptance, and general low self estimate is all a reflection of what needs to be healed deep within. That is the premise that I believe impacts many African Americans. For healing to be real to such individuals, the source of pain must be recognized, entered into one's consciousness and affirmed as real. Acceptance of the reality is not to diminish one's strength and personal fortitude, especially in the light of all that "we have gone through". Rather, it is conforming to the adage "You cannot solve a problem until you admit the problem exists". To review the historical impact of culture and society on African American life is to admit that there is something askew, albeit mostly out of our control, our response to it is completely within our control. That, to me, is the perspective that leads to healing. Wrong in this sense does not mean believing that what hurts me is insoluble or that it will take years and great effort to solve. It positions me to see it for what it is – to be absolved of what I am not responsible for, and to affirm what I am responsible for and to ultimately find the healing that I need.

To appropriate greater understanding of the helpfulness of this process, I want to share Michael's story.

Michael's Story

Michael (not his real name) is a 46 year old African American client who has a history of transitional employment, broken relationships and substance abuse. While he has been reluctant to call his life situation what it is – highly charged with dysfunction. Michael has recognized that something is seriously wrong. He admits that there are destructive patterns in his life that compromise his well being and actually keeps others at a distance from him. Often unable to accept any responsibility for his choices and the resultant cycles of dysfunction he finds himself in, Michael has decided he needs help. The following is his story.

My father was always very distant. I am not sure why. It seemed to me that he disliked my very existence. I am not sure why that is either. I remember how desperately I would try to please him. I would work on cars – no aptitude for it, but it was what he did – what he thought all 'boys' should do. I did reasonably well in school, but that didn't get me any points either. Most often there was no praise, no job well done. Usually it was more or less, what was expected of me – to do well. I always felt like I didn't fit in – actually hated for even being alive.

My father had big strong arms. He had big hands. I wondered what it would be like for him to hug me. I remember when I was little, not sure how old I was, I fell from a broken step on Grandma's porch. I banged my knee up pretty badly and the blood scared me more than anything else. I was really crying. Someone got my father. It was his mother's house. Before he checked me out he told me "stop crying"! Bellowing "are you a punk or something"? – "as big as you are, you have no business crying over this small cut." Several hours and six stitches later, the only thing I could think of was crying because I was hurt, meant that I must be a punk. For boys, no matter what, crying is not allowed.

It was allowed for him to strike me with his big hands, which he had done many times and threatened to do again if I had not stopped crying. To cry meant I was a sissy. Being a sissy, or at least being called one, was even worse than crying.

I carried that message with me from that day. I made it a point of not crying or showing any emotions whenever I was hurt. Even though I can recall many situations that hurt my feelings, I was not about to let anyone know that. Daddy would say such hurtful things, especially in front of my cousins and friends. It was like he really hated me!

My cousins and play mates laughed at me often, bellowing the mean and surly things they had heard from my father and siblings. Fearful of being picked on more, I was not a great athlete, like many of them. I could not play ball, or at least I didn't really try. I would run from a fight when picked on, mostly because everyone expected me to get beat up and to be the victim of more taunts and jeers. I could not be the leader of the pack, because no one ever wanted me in their gang. I never understood what it was about me that made no one ever choose me. But as I grew older, I began to create a world of my own, where I was safe, where I was accepted and no one laughed at me. I left home as soon as I graduated and never looked back. I was in and out of relationships with men and women. I traded pleasing them in any way imaginable, for their acceptance. I experimented with all kinds of drugs in all kinds of settings with the people I hooked up with. And when they would be cruel to me, or found someone else who could please them better I was either kicked to the curb, or ostracized. I would not fight for a relationship. I would suck it up – not cry – that was not allowable. I was a man. But, there was an inner loneliness in me that made me keep seeking something to fill the hole in my soul.

I have always had difficult relationships with men. Either I distanced myself from men altogether because they come across so aggressively or I find myself coming dangerously close to connecting with men of questionable character – men who would go out of their way to befriend me – who would draw me into things I really did not want to do, sometimes sexual things, only for me to feel even worse later, and to distance myself even more from men. Suspicious, non-trusting and fearful that I was becoming something I did not want to be, I would often be drawn back into such friendships because at the time they felt good and I felt good.

It was not much different with women. The women I became involved with were, many times, so eager to tell me how to live, and who to be, that I did not allow myself to live into an easy rhythm of man-woman friendship. It was so easy to let women take the lead. I would just follow, until their demands stirred the feelings in me that reminded me of how badly I felt when my mother criticized and judged me for not being able to 'do anything right'.

So here I am now, with a failed marriage after14 years, a son who despises me, two daughters who refer to me as 'him' and parents who still blame me for everything that has ever gone wrong in my life, and theirs! So I drink – a lot! I do not and cannot take life seriously. Life has never been serious about me. And, not only do I drink, but I have been known to do the harder stuff if I felt really pressured. And there are other things that I do which feel good at the time – things that I am too ashamed to even talk about – things that if the right people knew about, whoever the right people are, they would make sure my life would be ruined altogether.

So I hide from myself. I pretend a lot and I do what I do, to do what I do. I try not to question, telling myself "it is what it is". But I can't help but wonder, does it have to be this way? Is there not something more? Can I be more, have more, do more? Inadequate in relationships, disappointing as a husband and father and not really that successful in my career, what am I supposed to do?

On top of all the stuff that nobody really knows that goes on in my life, I call myself a Christian. By the standards of the folk who know me at church, I am. I am a deacon. I sing in the choir. I pray for people and even testify in church to the goodness of the Lord. However none of them know what lurks below the surface of my life. If I didn't know any better I would say God has given up on me too! But then, maybe I don't know better. Maybe He has. I still pray and I believe in miracles. I am just not sure there is a miracle for me. This stuff has been with me a long time.

I never thought about my father's passive behavior towards me as abusive or as a contributing factor to the many relationships I would later fail at. For that matter, I never thought about my mother's over controlling behavior towards me as damaging either. I never questioned the way things were because I didn't know they should have been or could have been any way other than the way they were.

I was watching a TV program – *Flight of the Concords* when something clicked inside of me. One of the lead characters, Jermaine said, "It doesn't matter what country someone's from, or what they look like, or the color of their skin. It doesn't matter what they smell like, or that they spell words slightly differently-some would say, more correctly. I'm a person. Bret's a person. You're a person. That person over there is a person. And each person deserves to be treated like a person." I just want to be a real person to somebody.

Life Application

"I do not understand what I do. For what I want to do I do not do, but what I hate I do." Romans 7:15 (NIV)

Unpacking Michael's Story

Michael suffers from a failure of self-esteem. The fact is that this failure is no fault of his own, largely stemming from the lack of love and acceptance he deserved from his parents as their child. From his earliest development Michael had not felt that his world was a welcoming and inviting place. Never having known his father's love and acceptance, and mostly experiencing domination and control from his mother – out of a God birthed core longing, Michael has sought substitutes to meet the deep need of his life – love.

Equally, Michael has not been affirmed for the wonderful gift he is. Without affirmation during his critical years of development he has sought affirmation in dysfunctional ways, through equally broken individuals who were not capable of meeting his emotional need. He did not want to engage in dysfunctional behaviors that would ultimately shame him and fill him with guilt, but he knew of no other pathway for fulfillment and validation.

In the truest sense, Michael's is a sin problem, but underneath the occasions of sin in Michael's life is a God-given core longing. These longings deserve legitimate attention if Michael is to ever find wholeness. As a Christian, raised in a Christian home, Michael has never given himself permission to accept that many of his parents' actions toward him were also a result of their own sinfulness. Out of their brokenness, they wounded Michael. Out of Michael's wounding, to anesthetize his pain and to inoculate himself against further pain, Michael engaged in sinful behaviors, symptomatic of his dysfunction.

In Romans 7, Paul describes himself as "sold under sin." He identifies himself as one that is a slave to sin. One who is not free; one who, no matter how hard he tries to do good, captured by sin, invariably he does wrong. Sin, as captor holds him in vise like chains. Through the lens of 'slavery' Michael has to see his dysfunction. As an African American, his history alone puts his predicament in perspective. Michael must accept two truths. First, when one is not free, he can only do what his captors warrant. Second, when one is not free, he only realizes his need for liberation when his captor, that which has enslaved him, begins to rob him of his life.

In Paul's testimony, he makes the point to the Jews that living under the law means being a slave to sin. Sin is a merciless taskmaster. As a slave, sin has robbed you of your life. But the good news is that there is a liberator. There is one who frees from sin. He has the power. He is the Messiah, the one through whom victory is possible under grace. The law was never meant to save us from sin. Only Jesus can do that. He has done that by the power of His cross.

Michael needs to know that in the deepest part of himself, he is so worthy of love that flows from the glorious cross of Christ. He needs to know, to hear the Lord pronounce him free of guilt and shame, that there is nothing wrong with him that grace has not made provision for. Despite what he did or did not get from his parents the arms of the Lord Jesus are stretched wide to fully and lovingly embrace Michael without judgment, without chastisement, and without recrimination. The cross of Christ is the remedy for sin and it is more powerful than Michael's dysfunction.

Re-visiting the Structures of Healing

In Michael's life situation, the observable level of the Structures of Healing, Michael is acting out the pain of his most recent failed relationship. He is uncomfortable with being alone and needs another person's presence in his life to feel valid and complete. Yet, when you meet Michael, one sees an exterior of cool toughness with an almost angry affect of guardedness and inapproachability.

Since his current relationship breakup, he is angry over the fact that he has been drinking more, visiting questionable social networks, and engaging in behaviors that shame him. Shame-filled, he is not able to look deeply at what is underneath his behavior. He fears to look to closely he will discover that all of the hurtful and ugly things he has believed about himself are true. What Michael has not come to terms with, what he has never been introduced to is the truth of who he is. It is important that Michael tells his story. That is the first step towards his healing.

In unpacking his story, I am able to help Michael see the relationship between his life situation, and the underlying dysfunctional behaviors that he engages in to make himself feel better. Desiring his father's love and acceptance and the experience of living with a critical and domineering mother, Michael believed he was not worthy of love and acceptance. In fact, Michael believed something was "wrong" with him. He believed that feeling was validated in the way he related to his peers. In his peer relationships he always felt rejected.

When his peers made fun of him, it tapped into the place of wounding causing him to retreat even deeper into his pain. Becoming stoic and detached, he showed little emotion or passion for life. Yet, it was clear to me that out of his "inner loneliness" he wanted acceptance, love and inclusion.

Going deeper, I am able to help Michael connect his behaviors with uncomfortable feelings that stir in him when his world and wellbeing is threatened. It is out of this emotional upheaval, that Michael defaults to past behaviors that have made him feel better in times of emotional pain.

Only a temporary reprieve, Michael must get in touch with what drives what he believes about himself. He must dislodge the lies rooted in a significant wounding experience that has shaped his beliefs about himself and his perspective on his life.

In a sense, I need to help Michael identify the ground that has been conceded to sin birth out of Michael's brokenness. The goal of formational prayer is certainly to position people for a transforming encounter with Christ in the places of their deepest pain and greatest dysfunction. I want to suggest what that change will look like against the backdrop of the structure that was just defined.

Before encountering the Lord through inner healing prayer the person's issues move from wound, to false beliefs, to emotional upheaval, to dysfunctional behavior, all of which are acted out in the life situation.

Through the ministry of the Holy Spirit a significant change takes place in this pattern. The wound becomes a place where the person meets the Lord and experiences His empowering grace. The lies are now replaced by the truth of who they are in Christ Jesus, which brings a significant amount of comfort and peace even in the midst of life's difficulties and trials.

This peace then enables them to experience empowered living which is lived out within the individual's life situation – illustrated on the following page.

STRUCTURES OF HEALING
(Wardle, *Healing Care, Healing Prayer*, 2001)

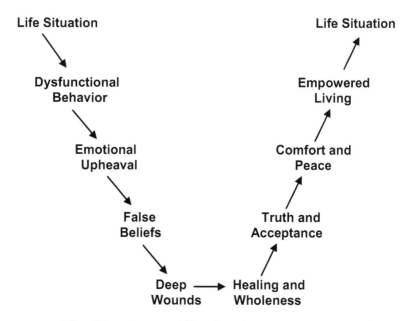

The Structures of Healing is a starting place for unveiling the places where you may be stuck, and for examining your life response to the underlying issues that most often are not in your awareness. To decide to look at your life through this lens is to move from indecision to appropriate actions that will allow you to trust God for the wholeness and fullness of life that He promises. Entering in, you are invited to live into the story of your life with the possibility that God can edit, not undo, but edit the painful places so that with clarity you can see your way through the maze. Doing this, perhaps you will find that there is a balm in Gilead; there is a physician here; the Lord is in Zion.

Chapter Seven

No One Really Cares About My Feelings

When You Can't Get a Prayer Through

April 4, 2007, Don Imus, of MSNBC's *Imus in the Morning Show*, referred to the Rutgers University's women's basketball team, which is comprised of eight African-American and two white players, as "nappy-headed hos". After African American activists across the country threatened to boycott CBS Radio and MSNBC, the racist comment ultimately resulted in Don Imus' termination on CBS radio and the MSNBC simulcast. However, this was not before Imus reached a multimillion-dollar settlement with CBS over his firing and the possibility that he could return to broadcasting as early as January, 2008.

The star center for the Rutgers women's basketball team, Kia Vaughn, filed a lawsuit against Imus for libel, slander, and defamation. She sought monetary damages on the basis that referring to women on the team as "nappy headed" was debasing, demeaning, humiliating, and denigrating to Vaughn and her fellow players. Her lawyer, Richard Ancowitz, speaking to ABC News contended that "there's no way these bigoted remarks should have seen the light of day."[37]

The lawsuit alleged that ABC and MSNBC 'wrongfully, intentionally, willfully ... created, tolerated and maintained an atmosphere in which the making of outrageous statements and comments was acceptable, encouraged, and/or rewarded for many years prior to this occurrence and/or overtly encouraged the statements made.' That settlement, said Ancowitz, rewards Imus while leaving little justice for the women of the Rutgers basketball team. "He's come out smelling like quite the rose. But what about these young women? How does Imus' victory affect their self-esteem? Where do they go to get their reputations back?" [38]

The real question is why was it acceptable for such a comment to be made in public media in the first place? The answer is simple, it is this, at a primal level there are still deeply held feelings, negative stereotypes, and misrepresentations about race that have been generalized and acceptable to the majority culture in American life. Because of this generalized acceptance, race is the dividing line that distinguishes us. In many unmonitored moments it is conceivable that caustic comments will come from deeply held unchallenged feelings and beliefs that are all rooted in racism.

---

[37] http://www.eonline.com/uberblog/b56151_rutgers_player_drops_imus_suit.html

[38] http://query.nytimes.com/gst

The purpose of the lawsuit was about restoring the good name and reputation of "my client, Kia Vaughn, and the other 12 players of the team" said her attorney, Richard Ancowitz, in an exclusive interview with the ABC News Law & Justice Unit.[39]

Vaughan had spoken out about Imus on Oprah Winfrey's talk show in April 2007, stating that Imus' comments had overshadowed the teams remarkable season. She received no support from the Rutgers women's basketball coach, or her other teammates – the majority of whom were African American. The University made no comment on the lawsuit. A furor of opinions and blogs erupted around the lawsuit filed by Vaughan with comparisons of Imus' comments to "Hip Hop" claiming that his comments were no more inflammatory or berating. There were those who readily acknowledged how wrong and unwarranted these comments were. Nonetheless, against the backlash of criticism and media attention, citing revenge as the motive for Vaughan's lawsuit, *The New York Times* reported that Ms. Vaughn withdrew her suit and returned to Rutgers to focus on completing her journalism degree and playing basketball with her teammates.[3]

Is there no injury here? Does anyone care about the feelings, the pain that these young women suffered because of such derogation? A longstanding belief in the African American community is that there is no reparation. No one cares about your injuries or your feelings for that matter. Society doesn't care, and

---

[39] http://mediamatters.org/research/200704040011

in most instances neither does your cultural community. Is it that we are so desperate to be included and accepted that we even snub our nose at the things that create pain for us and the things that ostracize and exclude us?

Looking closely at the Rutgers situation it is clearly determinable that Vaughan and her friends felt the odds were against them. Fearing reprisal none of the other African American female athletes joined her in her suit, with no support from the coach or the University for whom the team played an amazing season. Imus is fired, receiving a multimillion dollar settlement, but Vaughan and her teammates walk away carrying the stigma of a stereotype that eclipses the significance of their accomplishments and denigrates them personally.

Under New York law, a defamation claim fails if "either the full context of the communication in which the statement appears or the broader social context and surrounding circumstances are such as to signal readers or listeners that what is being read or heard is likely to be opinion, not fact." [40] So, from a point of law there is yet again support for such experiences and incidents. Albeit obviously and systemically racist, It perpetuates the feeling that the culture does not care. You can produce for the culture, according to the culture's expectations, but the culture places no value on your personage, only on what you can produce. Many African American athletes can tell this story.

---

[40] Brian versus Richardson, 87 N.Y. 2d 46 (1995) 660 N.E. 2d, 1126

In his book *Standing in the Shadows*, John Heard argues that the problem of ignoring feelings and emotions in African American men can be traced back to slavery, when it was believed that blacks were unable to feel inner pain because they had no psyche.[41] As a result of such beliefs, many African Americans internalize their feelings, not willing to risk castigation by society in general but specifically by fellow African Americans, they tell themselves – do not feel. Head argues that this myth has damaged generations of African American men and their families and has created a society that blames black men for being violent and aggressive without considering that depression may actually be the root cause. The onset of this depression stems from the inability to talk about one's inner pain.

Similarly, Terrie Williams in her 2005 book *Black Pain: It just looks like we're not hurting*, explores depression in Black America, beginning with her own personal experience. The following excerpt of an interview with Williams in the August, 2005 issue of *Ebony* is compelling. Describing the extreme reticence of African Americans to talk about issues that hurt – emotional issues – of things experienced, felt, believed – Williams suggests that the majority of dysfunctional behavior and the subsequent depression that is not talked about in the African

---

[41] Heard, John. 2004. *Standing in the Shadows: Understanding and Overcoming Depression in Black Men,* Portland Oregon: Broadway Books

American community is the end result of suffering in silence.[42]

> EBONY: The details of BLACK PAIN are raw. Are you sounding the alarm bell?
>
> WILLIAMS: Black people from all walks of life are enduring crippling emotional challenges that cause thousands of us to suffer from depression. Most of us do not have a clue what's causing some of our severe health problems, such as high blood pressure and heart disease. We don't understand why we don't have the strength to get out of bed, or why we feel suicidal, when from [the] outside [it looks as if] we have everything to live for. Depression plays a major role in every aspect of social misery, domestic and street violence, and child abuse. The list is endless ... There isn't one among us on the planet who is not dealing with the pain and disappointments we inherit from our parents and some childhood scars we have not spoken about. Many of those issues are keeping us from being our best selves and doing what we were called to do. We must begin to deal with these issues in order to grow. That's one reason, among many, why I wrote BLACK PAIN.
>
> EBONY: What was the turning point for you in dealing with your own depression?
>
> WILLIAMS: Coming out of the nine months of a devastatingly crippling depression. That was really the turning point for me--and that I am sitting here

---

[42] Permission to include this excerpt granted by Ebony

today clothed and in my right mind talking with you (laughing). When I finally did share my story, I got over 10,000 letters from people telling me something about themselves that family and their best friends didn't know. That's depression. They were either suffering with some kind of pain, mental or physical, or there was something holding them back and they didn't recognize the symptoms. During this period of suffering, you lie because you don't know what's going on, or you're too embarrassed to tell anyone. You show up late to work, or you're absent, or unproductive. You're the walking wounded. That's the hidden face of depression that I'm trying to reveal.

EBONY: What can be done to help people?

WILLIAMS: Awareness, awareness--awareness [Help] begins there. I deliberately wrote BLACK PAIN in very accessible language and reached out to real people, from [the celebrity] to the business professional to the gang-banger. My goal is for anyone who reads the book to see themselves, or someone that they know, and [letting them know] they are not on the ledge alone; they don't have to wear a mask. When we try to deny our true feelings, we become prisoners in our own mind ... it's dangerous ... We must share our stories with each other.

EBONY: Who is the target audience for the book?

WILLIAMS: I'd have to say that all Black people will benefit from the book because even if you don't personally suffer from depression, you know someone who [is suffering from the disease].

Problem is, they [are likely suffering in silence]. How many times do we write people off as "evil" or "crazy" and wind up avoiding them all together? ... I just want us to know what to look for.

Both Heard and Williams have done extensive research into the issues of pain and brokenness within the African American community. Focusing largely on depression, they bring to light the tendency of African Americans to hide and ignore symptoms of depression, which in many instances stem from inequitable opportunities, a sense of hopelessness, and a general feeling that the world is against them.

The feelings of sadness, energy loss, even thoughts of death or suicide are not taken seriously because of the overall "survival" makeup of most African Americans. Couple this with the misgivings that many African Americans have about mental health services, it is a wonder that there has not been breakdown of epidemic proportion in the African American community.

There is contravening intervention, an option to suffering in silence. That option is formational prayer – turning to the God who loves, hears, and understands. It is not God's will that you bear and bear and bear all the pain and brokenness put upon you as a result of the pain and brokenness of others. That's what racism is at its root – the brokenness of others, even the brokenness of systems and institutions which are commanded by broken individuals.

It has been the philosophy of many African Americans to *"bear our burdens in the heat of the day knowing that the Lord will make a way"*, a song often sung with deep heartfelt conviction that unfavorable circumstances will change, if you bear up under them long enough. Such "bearing" eventually becomes an insufferable weight and heavy yoke, making it difficult to pray – "to get a prayer through". God says "Cast your cares on me for I care for you" (I Peter 5:7 NIV). God says, "Come to me, all you who are weary and burdened. Take my yoke upon you and learn from me, for I am gentle and humble in heart, and you will find rest for your souls" (Matthew 11:28, 29 NIV). God says, "Give me your heavy yoke" and I will give you an easy yoke, I will bear your burdens as you are yoked with me.

At a surface glance the imagery of a yoke looks more like bondage and diminished freedom placed on us by one with power over us. But Jesus is saying "yoke with me" – not a single yoke, but a double yoke, where He journeys in tandem with us. It is like the double yoked oxen working together to accomplish a task. The two together decrease the load for each other. It is this kind of yoke that Jesus is talking about. A yoke that we don't have to pull alone, he wears it with us. It is not a yoke of servitude, or bondage, but it is a yoke of connection. It is a way of being in relationship with Christ that eclipses the difficulty of life – not making life more difficult. It is in this kind of relationship that Christ comes alongside us. In true and authentic communion he helps us know the difference between circumstances that can deepen us in him, and circumstances that can deaden us, distancing us even more from God's love.

Life Application

Why is it Difficult for Blacks to Honestly, Authentically Share their feelings?

Suppose black men were suffering through an epidemic. What if the disease struck as many as 20 percent of all African American men during their lives, and what if 15 percent of those with the most severe strain of the illness died? Imagine that the disease made men miss work, and made them less motivated and productive when they were on the job. Imagine further that even black men at the top of their professions were affected, rendered less decisive, their judgment impaired. And what if, in an effort to ease the pain of the disease, many African American men medicated themselves with addictive, deadly drugs? What if black families were being destroyed by this illness? What if many of the men suffering from this disease lost hope so completely that they placed little value on human life-theirs or anyone else's? And, finally, what if, while all this was happening, next to nothing was being done... [43]

---

[43] Heard, John. 2004. *Standing in the Shadows: Understanding and Overcoming Depression in Black Men,* Portland Oregon: Broadway Books

There are many causes of depression. The physiological causes of depression usually result when certain brain neurotransmitters are not secreted in sufficient amounts to alleviate mood disorders. The chemical's serotonin, melatonin, and dopamine are the most important to our sense of well being. When the nerves are robbed of these neurotransmitters, they cannot send messages to other nerves, and depression results.

Psychologically, our personalities have a lot to do with our sense of wellbeing. Individuals who were abused in childhood may not be very resilient and these individuals may become overly dependent on others. Those who are prone to see life as hopeless and unfair may also tend toward depression. For example, if repetitive life circumstances convince an individual that he or she is deserving of pain, and disappointment, that person may tend towards depression.

Socially, an individual who may be predisposed depression can sometimes rise above it. However, it is far more likely, that being abused, poor, neglected, or separated from loved ones will encourage an already burgeoning depression.

In many instances the onset of depression results from a sense of being unwanted, not needed and devalued, experiencing sustained duress, or chronic pain or illness that creates a sense of hopelessness and despair. At its extreme, depression can become a debilitating mental disorder.

Much of what is experienced as depression stems from unresolved painful emotional issues and experiences that have been masked and ignored. These experiences, which compromise wellbeing and erode self-esteem, are really messengers that call attention to our need for healing. If one engages in self-medicating, or other means of escaping the emotional pain one may fall prey to depression which can exacerbate physical symptoms.

Why is it difficult for blacks to open up, to share the places of pain in their life that can lead to the greater pain of depression? I think the answer to this question lies in the belief that "no one is to be trusted". This is a core belief held by many African Americans. It is forged out of a history of oppression and many experiences of betrayal.

Beginning with the slave trade a history of oppression was set in motion, in this country, that created fear and suspicion causing African Americans to suppress their feelings and emotions. It was much easier to act in a way that "master" found acceptable. So doing, reduced the possibility of abuse, beatings and possibly even being sold. It made life easier. The drawback to this was what was initially engineered as a method of self protection, from "master's" harshness, carried forth to present times.

As African Americans continued, even after slavery, to find themselves treated with disdain and disrespect, to make their lives easier they spoke and acted the way they believed made them more acceptable by the dominant culture. Masking their "true self", their thoughts and emotions because of the disrespect and humiliation they constantly received, they hid their frustration and anger from their oppressor and from each other. They understood that revealing their true feelings was at great risk and possibly even greater loss.

As time grew on, this "masking" was not only self protecting, but a behavior that was designed to keep African Americans from carrying each other's pain. Blacks refused to impose their deep pain and anxiety upon their loved ones because, for the most part, their loved ones were in pain themselves. It was this kind of mindset that caused blacks to draw on the only strength they had left: determination and spirituality. While withholding their emotional selves from one another, they knew that God would hear their prayers. So in praying, telling God about their pain, they found comfort believing there was going to be a day of reckoning and even retribution.

Paul Laurence Dunbar, son of slave parents, was a brilliant student who penned the words to the poem "We Wear the Mask." In high school, Dunbar worked as an elevator operator. His poem was in response to his experiences and treatment as a young African American striving for a place in culture. The poem expresses the pain and torment of African-Americans, describing the source of their strength as being from God while relying upon their inner faith and might to persevere; they refused to appear weak to those who berated and denigrated them – even to each other! Just as the child who closes his eyes believes himself to be invisible, hiding behind the "mask" meant no one could see them for who they really were or connect with the pain they really felt.

WE WEAR THE MASK
Paul Laurence Dunbar (1872-1906)

We wear the mask that grins and lies,
It hides our cheeks and shades our eyes--
This debt we pay to human guile;
With torn and bleeding hearts we smile
And mouth with myriad subtleties.

Why should the world be over-wise,
In counting all our tears and sighs?
Nay, let them only see us while
We wear the mask.

We smile, but oh great Christ, our cries
To Thee from tortured souls arise.
We sing, but oh the clay is vile
Beneath our feet, and long the mile;
But let the world dream otherwise,
We wear the mask![44]

---

[44] Dunbar, Paul L. 1993. *The Complete Poems of Paul Laurence Dunbar*. New York: Dodd, Mead, and Co.

Chapter Eight

Singing in a Minor Key

"A bird sang sweet and strong
In the top of the highest tree,
He said, "I pour out my heart in song
For the summer that soon shall be."

But deep in the shady wood,
Another bird sang, "I pour
My heart on the solemn solitude
For the springs that return no more."

– George William Curtis

In worship, we are an emotive people. It is not unusual to enter a euphoric African American worship service where feelings and heightened emotions, invoking the presence of God punctuate the atmosphere. Especially this is true at the "Altar Call" – the prayer moment. Individuals 'call out' – no in some instances, "cry out" to God for themselves and for each other. Simultaneously lamenting an injustice, confessing the ache of intractable pain, worshippers enlist the support of the gathered church to assail the gates of heaven for a decisive and victorious move of God in insufferable situations. Sometimes with deep feelings of sadness and at other times rippled with a sense of anger and unfairness, the "prayer request" riveted with great detail, draws the faithful worshipers into the individual's pain and brokenness. And, they pray 'breakthrough' prayers until they can leave the altar filled with praise, declaring in a united chorus… "I've got a feeling everything's gonna be alright."

At various places in African American worship, pain and struggle is legitimized as the heart is focused on God's role in the rightness, wrongness, goodness, or badness, of the worshiper's situation. So with passion, one cries out to God. For many African Americans, this is the counseling office. It is a cultural expectation that one can "take their burden to the Lord, and leave it there." Seldom are African Americans open to talking to a counselor about their troubles. Most often, with little hesitation, African Americans open their souls to God in heart-felt, deeply personal and sometimes, very desperate, prayer. In our songs, we join together and sing of our struggles. Our music depicts a deep faith and belief that even if nothing is done about it right away, God is not going to forsake the righteous forever. In the 'call and response' of our worship, testimony and sermon alike allows for pain and joy to be shared, surrendered to God, hope is retrieved in God's faithfulness.

In, *Wade in the Water,* Arthur Jones, a black psychologist talks about the spirit of African American worship as a recapturing of the heart of the "sorrow songs" of the Negro Spirituals. The songs are reflective of the anguish and hope of the heart. They are deeply personal songs that look to God for intervention, for help, for liberation and deliverance. And, these songs, formed in trial and persecution are descriptive of the African American experience and culture altogether. W.E.B. Du Bois said,

> Through all of the Sorrow Songs there breathes a hope-a faith in the ultimate justice of things. The minor cadences of despair change often to triumph and calm confidence. Sometimes it is faith in life, sometimes a faith in death, sometimes assurance of boundless justice in some fair world beyond. But whichever it is, the meaning is always clear: that sometime, somewhere, men will judge men by their souls and not by their skins. [45]

In his observance of African American worship and the power of lament, Dan Allender shares similar thoughts as DuBois. He writes,

> Many individuals know deep suffering. But few have been part of a culture that is defined by sorrow. If one reads, or listens to the art of these cultures, one is led not to despair, but to passionate hope. It is far from what we expect.

---

[45] Arthur C. Jones. 1993. *Wade in the Water: The Wisdom of the Spirituals, p. 18.* Maryknoll: Orbis Books

But I would argue the greatest power in art, life, and faith comes from the soil of lament. Lament embodies the passions of need, the fight against injustice, and implicitly the loudest proclamation of hope. [46]

Lamenting is very much a part of the African American experience of God. God is never credited for our troubles but He is often questioned – "how long." So we sing in a minor key, sometimes dirge-like, sometimes with great anguish and tears, but always filled with hope – we sing.

The traditional Negro Spiritual, *Sometimes I feel like a motherless child, a long way from home*, echoes the pathos of the African American soul. It is a lament. It is a truth that resonates with the places of mistreatment, inhumanity and deep brokenness shaped by a society that says you don't belong, you have no place at the table. It is out of the pain and struggle that we grope to find God. Lamenting, accesses that place in a way that no counseling encounter can. It is the refrain of the psalmist, "Will the Lord reject forever? Will he never show his favor again?" (Psalm 77:7).

To sing in sorrow is to befriend one another and to authenticate that we are ultimately not alone, even if no one can fully comprehend our pain now.

---

[46] Allender, Dan. 1994. *The Hidden Hope in Lament*. Mars Hill Review, 1 (1)

The awareness that we are not alone increases our courage to honestly look at the pain and to struggle to know God in the midst of it all. It gives us less excuse to withdraw from fellowship assuming either no one understands me, or everyone else has his or her life in order. Those assumptions destroy the integrity of true Christian community.[47]

Let me affirm this place of growth in the soul's journey. Continue to sing in the minor key, we are a long way from home – not just the eternal home that we long for, but from 'being at home' fully in the earth. Whether we sing in the choir of familiar voices who give witness to the longing for justice, peace, mercy, deliverance, or whether we sing solo from anguish birthed in the deepest recesses of a soul that longs for vindication – God honors your lament. God hears your cry and it is not in vain.

Life Application

You Better Cry Boy!

As a boy growing up, when my mother would discipline me, I was not sure how I was supposed to respond to the discipline. As I grew older, because of the message that boys are not supposed to cry, when

---

[47] Op. cit.

she would discipline me, especially if it was with a belt or switch (back in the day that was acceptable), I was hard pressed to know whether or not it was ok to cry. But my mother was classic. As she would go through her lecture leading up to the punishment, she would say, "I am going to whip you, and you better not cry." But as she would get into the rhythm of her disciplining it was not unlike her to yell, "you better cry boy" to which I would immediately begin to wail and scream as if life itself was being drawn from me! Now this was very schizophrenic, you might say. Which is it? Do I cry, or don't I?

It didn't take long for me and my six siblings to realize that, while momma wanted us to grow up and learn to face the consequences of our wrong doings with some since of dignity and maturity, she did not feel triumphant in her lessons until she had heard the familiar wailings that assured her that her point had been made. So we learned quickly – after the third lick, scream like a banshee and cry as if you were on your last leg of life, she would go easier on you, feeling confident that you got it!

Now I am certain you find a little humor in this vignette from a scene in my childhood. You probably recall similar stories of your own. But there is something about crying that needs to be addressed. Healthy crying, crying that stems from loss, while largely discouraged in our world, is a necessary crying of healing tears. I see the need for such healing tears in Jason's life.

Jason always believed that crying was a sign of weakness. In fact he was told, that to display emotion of any kind was a sign of weakness. That is the message that most males receive especially African American males. And, when raised by a single parent that message is louder and clearer.

Jason was the only child born to his mother, and she had submerged herself into his world. She lived her life through him and he lived his life through her. Although Jason was well liked, very active in Church and had a good outlook on life, he did not readily make friends out of his loyalty to his mother. He had gotten the message that having friends was to dismiss his mother as significant in his life. She always reminded him that all they had was each other.

At age sixteen, Jason's mother, a long time diabetic, was stricken with an untreatable circulatory condition resulting from chronic diabetes. As her medical condition deteriorated she had to have her right leg amputated. After undergoing the surgery, the circulation problem persisted leading the doctors to conclude that in order for her to get better her left leg would also need to be removed. Stating that without this procedure his mother would possibly die, Jason and his aunt, his mother's only sister, consulted the doctors further. After confirming the diagnosis, his aunt told him, "Jason, you are a man, you need to make the decision for what is best for your mom."

In talking with his mother, she pleaded that she did not want the surgery - she would take her chances without it. Jason, without any observable emotion, convinced her that the surgery would be the best course of action. Reluctantly consenting to the surgery, his mother sank into a deep depressive state. The surgery required radical amputation leaving his mother semi-invalid. She never emerged from the deep sadness and depression over her loss. She felt useless. She now believed herself to be a burden to Jason – something she never wanted. After all, they only had each other and it was her job to take care of him, not vice versa. Within two weeks of the surgery, Jason's mother died. Overwrought with grief, it was as if she surrendered her will to live so as not to become a burden to her son. Jason was overcome with sadness, it was clear that he was hurting badly, but he would not cry.

Prior to her death, Jason had become reclusive and difficult to engage. His conversation, which was usually light and enthusiastic – filled with warmth and receptivity, had become darkened with brooding and foreboding. His affect, dull and sullen, became worse after his mother's funeral. At the funeral he showed no emotion, with the exception of a slight tear just as his mother's body was being committed to the grave. He could not leave the funeral brunch soon enough.

He didn't want to hear condolences, nor did he want to be forced to respond to perfunctory expressions by individuals who he felt really did not care. He left the funeral brunch without saying very much to anyone.

Some months later I saw Jason, dark, unfriendly, and detached. With a pallor of sadness characterizing his affect, he was difficult to engage, and responded to my greeting, and inquiry with short matter-of-fact phrases. It was as if he was angry with the world, but he was not going to let the world know it. He would not talk about his mother's sickness, her subsequent death, or her funeral, insisting that there was nothing to talk about. It was clear that Jason was not willing to give himself permission to grieve.

No one cared for Jason like his mother. His father abandoned him at birth and no matter how much he tried to have a relationship with him Jason experienced one rejection after another from him. When his mother died, his world collapsed around him. He felt alone, unprotected and afraid. He masked this through presenting a tough, untouchable façade that conveyed to the casual onlooker that he didn't need anyone, or anything least of all he didn't need anyone to care about him.

He would not let himself cry, because he did not want to appear to be weak or to risk being taken advantage of if he showed any weakness. He was now thrust into an adult world to fend for himself. He could not allow himself to be vulnerable. He needed to be strong. That would be the only way he could make it. Now that his mother was gone he had to make sure he counted on no one but himself.

In talking with Jason, I wanted so much to touch that hurting place inside of him. Even more, I wanted him to trust the Lord to touch that tender place of pain. I shared with him that it was ok to cry, to grieve – that crying is generally a sign that one is experiencing something overwhelmingly emotional. It could be enormous joy, sorrow, fear, hopelessness, despair, grief, love, or even confusion. More importantly, I wanted him to understand that he had suffered a monumental loss, and that he was not under any obligation to be strong – that his fullest strength was found in grieving his loss and trusting God for renewed hope.

Jason's response was one of anger and resentment over the fact that I was trying to make him feel something that he insisted he did not feel. While every behavior, his affect, tone, speech and posture demonstrated just how deep was his anger and pain, it was clear that Jason saw grieving, specifically crying as a loss of capacity and strength. But there was the inner crying that could be traced on his face that let me know Jason felt like a victim, and he was hurting deeply.

Jason's unwillingness to grieve had so locked him into an internal battle of emotions that it began to take its toll on every relationship. He became caustic and bitter. He was unkind to those who reached out to him, became indifferent to the overtures of friendship and love, and in general became cynical and unpleasant to be around.

It actually takes a strong person to surrender to the overpowering emotions that mark one's life with the profound pain and sadness that stem from loss. Yet it is exactly when we surrender to the moment of that pain that God allows those very feelings to release a flood of His love washing over us. His love embraces us and in that moment takes us to a place in Himself that sets us on the path of His plan to heal us. The weak cannot tolerate such emotion and will most often do whatever they can to stuff, numb or hide their emotions. They do this usually through performance, abusing substances or even denial that is so forceful that it keeps others at a distance from them.

This is the good news. God welcomes our tears. He wants to cradle our grief and the pain that we experience when life's losses are so great. As African Americans, we have borne so many losses that we have excused, justified, denied – that we cast all losses into the same box and simple chalk them up as "life". But God is inviting us into a different journey, one where it is okay to cry, to say I hurt, to lament and to cry out to him about what is fair, or not fair; what is just or unjust. It is in this place of strength that we discover God's tenderness, His love, His compassion, His desire to hold us close.

Chapter Nine

When Home is Where Your Heart is Broken

Maurice, at age 14 came home to announce that he was no longer going to be a part of his family. He was tired of his father fighting his mother, tired of the arguing and screaming, tired of there never being a moment of peace and calm in his home – he never felt safe. His father seemed angry all the time. His mother seemed to always try to please his father, but nothing she ever did was enough. It was nothing for his dad to call her an ugly name or to berate her or put her down in some embarrassing way.

His older brother, Charles, stays out late. He breaks all the rules and when he does come home he is constantly arguing with both of his parents. They have no control over what he does. He has already stopped going to school and to talk about that is another fight. Maurice's little sister Charlotte 9 years old barely talk, and clutches him as if he is the only thing in the world she can hold onto. At school she isolates and detaches from the other students. The teachers have made every effort to assist Charlotte, but neither parent seems really interested in working with them to make things better for Charlotte.

Today, Maurice comes home from school. He enters his home through the front door and notices his mother sobbing. There is blood on the tissue she's holding. The boy starts to ask his mother why she is crying when he realizes what has happened. She answers his silent inquiry, quietly saying, "your dad ... he's on the back porch . . . he's had a bad day." Feeling helpless he goes to his room. From his window he can see his dad taking in the last swallow of beer and yelling, loud enough for the neighbors to hear, "Hey, bring me another beer. And where is that worthless son of yours? He was supposed to mow the lawn yesterday." Maurice, having seen this too many times before, leaves the house the way he came in. Two blocks down the street he is approached by a gang member and unceremoniously another child on the block has decided that gangs have something he wants and needs - a sense of belonging, acceptance. The gang becomes his family.

From this point on Maurice begins a life of trouble, compounding the difficulties he already experiences at home, He trades trouble and a life of crime and violence to fill his need for acceptance and belonging. The sadness is that everything Maurice really wanted was there in his family of origin, but they did not know that. So filled with deep need and brokenness themselves, they were neither present to

Maurice nor helpful in mending the brokenness of his soul.

Oddly enough, this was a family that went to church every Sunday. From the outside no one would have suspected the darkness that lurked behind their closed doors. No one would have imagined the degree of pain and longing locked away in their souls.

Yet, there are certain core needs that every person has in common, not just needs for food, water, and air, but core emotional needs like the need for acceptance and belonging – the need for love and understanding, that when met, tells a person he or she is of great worth and value.

This story is not an unfamiliar one in many African American homes. Nor is the dysfunction and violence isolated to a particular kind of household. Many African Americans feel a sense of existential despair and, inept to handle it, the effects of the despair is seen in the disruptive nature of the household.

The frustration that comes from the lack of economic parity is one source of this despair. Another source is what has been modeled and passed along generationally as a response to the feelings of helplessness when one cannot do as one would like for his or her family. The pattern of dysfunction that is ultimately sent to members of these households is that this is not a safe place, and no one really cares.

This is a pattern that many black families have lived into and their children become victims because they, like their parents, are in need of something that they cannot seem to find.

Maurice's home is characterized by anger, hostility and a constant inappropriate discharge of destructive emotions, usually aimed at the ones who really do love and care. But this family, especially the father, is responding to something deeper than the helplessness that is felt when one is trapped into a cycle of despair, and does not know how to get out of it. He is responding to the flood of emotions that have surfaced from a multitude of sources, all of which have created pain.

Whether it is a desperate father stricken by helplessness and the inability to cope with his own emotional deficits, compounded by a belief that the world is against him, or a son who, after getting the brunt of his father's pain, frustration and despair, who is himself hurting in the wake of such an exchange, the longing of their heart is the same. Both are longing to be understood, to be accepted, and to feel significance and worth.

It is like we're all on a search for this. We begin the search in the places where we think we can find what we need – home, with mom, dad, and siblings. But, when the need is not met there it is still no less a need. We then begin to search elsewhere for our needs to be met. In Maurice's case, it was a gang, and a life of aberrance and crime.

The truth is even in our families of origin, some of what we need to feel whole and complete will always be lacking. But that is not good news, simply because the hole in our soul is still there.

I have made a great discovery. The holes are designed for God to fill. When I need someone, God can satisfy. When I need acceptance, God says, He loves, He forgives and He accepts without condition. The desire for approval is one of the strongest desires we will ever know. Acceptance is a close second. Children want the approval of their parents. Teenagers want the approval of their peers. Husbands and wives want each other's approval. Even when we think that our greatest need is for love, love is ultimately expressed as approval. God says, I approve of you "whether you mow the yard or not", whether you get good grades or not – whether or not you are on the A team. God says, you are on my team and it doesn't get any better than that.

Next to approval, every person wants to feel safe. They want to feel secure. This is also a core emotional need – a core longing. Almost everything we do, even in the case with Maurice and his brother Charles, whether its staying out late or joining a gang, it all revolves around our need to feel safe and secure. This deep need alone shapes our actions, efforts, and desires.

When parents, in their own pain and from their own sense of hopelessness hurt each other, home is neither safe for them, nor for their children. Children need to have a sense of physical and emotional safety and security. Adults do too! When we feel this need most, God promises He will always be there. He can be counted on. He will never leave me or forsake us. So what we really need, is a real relationship with God, one where we can experience the fullness of who we are in Him, and learn how to appropriate that reality in times of despair.

Life Application

If Christ is All, Why do I long for More?

God designed us so that our soul is not happy until we are intimately connected with him. Deep within you is all that you need to trust God to meet your emotional needs and to begin a path of healthier living. On this path you will find greater fulfillment, and a desire to live your life more closely to the teachings of Jesus. Sadly, many individuals who are Christians have never developed a personal relationship with Christ so that He can actually be there for them, to help them in times of emotional crisis. In relationships like that, we put more trust and confidence in people than we do in God.

Unfortunately, without a real relationship with Christ, when people fail us, because they cannot meet our needs for whatever reason, we are left to nurse our pain with no resource for strength or help. Without an authentic relationship, you will always look for your needs to be met in people – people who inevitably will fail you because they, for the most part, have unmet needs just like you.

When we depend on people, rather than God, we will continually develop unhealthy relationships where we expect people to meet our deepest needs. When these unhealthy relationships fail us, we seek substitutes to make us feel better – we walk around, umbilical cord in hand, looking for someone or something to plug ourselves into. As a relationship with a parent and child requires a close bond, so does our relationship to Christ require a close bond.

To have a personal relationship with Jesus Christ involves interrelatedness between you and Christ. It is not the same as knowing about the Christ of history, or about being a part of a church. It is an experiential relationship between two persons, you and Jesus, that involves interaction, connection and communication. It is important to understand that a personal relationship with Jesus Christ is not just an objective relationship to the benefits that Christ made available by his death and resurrection. Without this type of relationship, you will always long for more. The problem is that you will not know what that "more" is or even what it is supposed to look like.

Only God can meet your deepest needs. He alone creates the pathway through which your core longings can be fulfilled. You cannot understand this until you live in Christ by faith. Only then will you have the spiritual understanding of the indwelling of the Spirit of Christ within our spirit (Rom. 8:9); that the living Lord Jesus Christ is in us (Col. 1:27; II Cor. 13:5). Christ is all. Without him you will long for more.

Begin studying the scriptures. You will discover that you are a son or daughter of God. That is your true identity. You will discover that God is holy, righteous and loving and that your true self is connected to the fact that God created you and loves you in spite of your sins. You are truly loved unconditionally. The Holy Spirit living in you is able to lead you, and guide you so that you can experience the fullest most abundant life possible.

As you call upon God in prayer, in the name of Jesus Christ, as you turn away from sin and accept God's grace – the forgiveness of sin, the life Christ won for you on the Cross, you will begin to notice changes in your life, even in your desires. That is because you are living in a real relationship with Christ. And, He is with you in every moment of pain and brokenness, in every obstacle that threatens your security and your acceptance in the beloved.

When you really love him, you can trust him to meet your deepest needs and to guide you to people who will sustain those needs as they, with you, reflect his love. What others say or do won't matter. You will feel good about yourself. You will see yourself as

God's dearly loved child, and as his child, you will rely fully on him for everything, including fulfilling the deepest core longings of your life. Once you understand the relationship between your core longings and your relationship with Christ, it becomes clear that God wants to fill the deepest longings of your heart.

Seeking approval, acceptance, or any other deep emotional need, outside of Christ will only leave you hungry and desperate for satisfaction. When you experience ridicule or rejection or those whom you believe should care for you disappoint you and hurt you, it disturbs your inner peace and causes you to question your identity – who you really are.

When your core longings are undermined, by those whom you believe should care, it ruptures your view of yourself, God and others. You then internalize your negative, hurtful experiences and seek to comfort yourself through dysfunctional behaviors. That was the plight of Maurice's family. The end result is that in your salient moments, you begin to doubt your personal worth and significance. You feel even worse.

Your security should never be tied to things or to people, or to anything that you could lose, but to who you are in Christ, God's child.

External approval is always reassuring. When we receive the validation of others it reinforces our view of ourselves. But our personal sense of self-worth should be built on the solid foundation of the finished work of Jesus Christ. Can you say yes to this truth, or is there yet more work in this area?

Look deep within, is Christ your intimate, personal friend? Do you regularly share conversation with Him through prayer and through his Word? Do you believe that He has a specific purpose for your life – that He has a future and a hope for you?

Chapter Ten

How Deep Is This Well?

When I was a boy I loved to watch the Tarzan movies on Saturdays. I remember how excited I would get when Tarzan would yell Oh-oh-ooo-oh-oh-oh-ooo . That was the signal that the bad guys were really going to get it! In most cases this also meant that I would be rooting for Tarzan to defeat, or even kill the black natives who were depicted as savage, wild, animal like beasts who were worthy of death. The more Tarzan would beat up the black natives, the more victorious I would feel that good had won, that right beat wrong, that justice had prevailed. And in those instances when the black natives, whom Tarzan had befriended, were in trouble, it was Tarzan who rescued them and made their world safe again.

In looking back, there are two observations that haunt me about my reaction to the Tarzan movies. First, I am now aware, in looking back, that I was cheering for my own defeat when Tarzan was killing the natives. They were black. Even at a very tender, vulnerable age, I had bought the lie that there was something untamed, savage, and wrong with being black. This was the picture painted by culture. And I bought it, hook, line, and sinker. Second, in the instances where the natives were rescued, they could only be 'rescued, or saved' by Tarzan, who was white. What is so hurtful about this realization is the degree to which this image has been deeply ingrained in the black psyche. The truth is, even in this present day, the ripples of this covert message prevail. There are some African Americans who have the "Tarzan" mentality seeing black as savage, untamed, unsophisticated and needing a "Tarzan" – the 'white man', to rescue them from the enemy. Tarzan is the key to their salvation.

Sadly, it has taken time, and will take more time still, for some of us to break free of these lies and their shaming effect on black minds. It takes time to reject the most important lie: that black people inherently can't do the same things white people can do, unless white people help them. So we reject our own giftedness and in the same measure, reject each other.

This rejection is a form of self-contempt, self-hatred that is demonstrated in how we live out of our sub-culture, preferring white day care facilities for our children to black day care facilities, believing that the white day care facility is better. This is a simple, yet poignant example of how deep this well is. The real truth is this; only black people can alter such thinking. It is more important than ever that we affirm our giftedness, the blessing of who we are, and our potential to bless one another. Then, we can begin to combat the negative, stereotypical images portrayed in culture about black people. The change begins with my personal affirmation of the truth of my own giftedness and being. Then that must be our collective affirmation too.

In 1966, Stokely Carmichael, writing for *The New York Review of Books* in which he tries to define "Black Power" reminds us, "from birth, black people are told a set of lies about themselves. We are told that we are lazy – yet I drive through the Delta area of Mississippi and watch black people picking cotton in the hot sun for fourteen hours. We are told, 'If you work hard, you'll succeed', but if that were true, black people would own this country. We are oppressed because we are black, not because we are ignorant, not because we are lazy, not because we're stupid (and got good rhythm), but because we're black."[48]

There is a barrage of lies that we as a people have believed about ourselves. And, what is even more perplexing is that in some instances, we have believed these lies about other blacks, but not about ourselves. This form of reflexive racism is also based on a lie. That lie is that some blacks are better than other blacks. This differentiation within the black community cannot be ignored. The well from which this pain is drawn is very deep. We cannot excuse

---

[48]Carmichael, Stokley. 1966. *Essay: Black Power.* New York Book Review

each other of the personal responsibility to face the truth – we are all black and equally gifted and wonderful. Much of what we believe about ourselves is the result of a stealthy system still deeply influenced by attitudes around race. When attention is called to this reality, rest assured, we will be accused of playing "the race card". In some instances this may be an excuse to camouflage irresponsibility, but in most instances it is not.

Like the Tarzan movies, black people have been plastered with negative images of themselves, so much so, that it is normative to accept these images as truth rather than to see them for what they are – racism in its most subtle and its most sophisticated form. The negative perceptions and the negative stereotypes of African Americans have been deliberately, sociologically and psychologically engrained so much so, that in large measure, it has given birth to an endorsement by blacks of what whites have contrived as a preferable perception of blackness. From skin tone to body image; from speech patterns to fashion and from educational accomplishment to social integration, these are lies we have believed.

Studies in social and economic inequality prior to the Civil Rights Movement indicate relative closeness of African Americans to each other. In a sense it was the *'black = black mindset'* that we looked at earlier, that shaped and influenced shared values, attitudes, and experiences. Because of the homogeneity of the African American community, blacks relied on each other for need satisfaction and social interaction.[49]

The Civil Rights movement advanced the possibility that blacks could 'get their share of the pie'. But it also gave rise to a stratification of the African American Community that actually militated against the closeness that otherwise marked African Americans as a people. Social stratification, the classification of people into groups based on shared socio-economic conditions, created a situation in which affluent blacks distanced themselves from blacks of lower socioeconomic backgrounds. Further, blacks who lived in predominantly white communities were even more likely to distance themselves from other blacks.[50] The researchers in this study determined that for African Americans raised in predominantly white environments, closeness to the larger African American community was contingent on the socialization messages provided by parents during important stages of identity development.

How deep is this well? Deep! And when you plumb the depths you will find it is deeper still. African Americans are weighed down with multiple layers of emotional baggage. There are the layers of self-acceptance and fear of rejection that must be waded

---

[49] Smith S., and Moore, M, Intraracial Diversity and Relations among African Americans. *American Journal of Sociology* Volume 106 Number 1 (July 2000): 1–39
[50] Ibid

through. Pleasing people and striving for perfection, within the subculture of the African American community, and in the cultural mainstream, masks the need to fit in; to belong; to be honored; to be recognized as valuable. These are deeply embedded layers of this intense emotional well. Just underneath these layers are fear, distrust, and anger. This well is very deep! And frequently rising to the surface is denial, the desire for retribution, and self deprecating behaviors that reflect varying degrees of self hatred.

Only in truth can we drill down deep enough to release the well-spring of God's grace and love that it may freely flow, carrying us in its stream to the place of healing. And if we are to be free to live in this place of grace and love, indeed, we must recognize, and address the many lies that we have believed, disputing them, replacing them with the truth of our preciousness.

Life Application

Relationships are a very valuable part of our lives, and God desires for us to have healthy, enjoyable relationships. As you seek to grow in your journey of healing, there are some cautions that must be heeded. In *The Search for Significance,* Robert McGee declares "we can build our self-worth on our ability to please others or on the love and forgiveness of Jesus Christ".[51] Looking at the relationship patterns, identified by McGee in this classic work, you will see broad descriptions of the characteristic behaviors of each pattern. Even though I contend that there are many external issues beyond our control that has impacted the wellbeing and societal adjustments of many African American people, I have discovered too that there are some truths about brokenness that are universal. The 'search for significance' is a universal journey. Because there is an inherent propensity to engage this search, I find McGee's insights to be very helpful for dismantling self-imposed barriers, resistance, and for challenging core beliefs that lead to compromised emotional and spiritual health. If you see yourself in any of these descriptions take a proactive stand for the truth. The Lord wants to meet you in these false beliefs. He has come, in Christ, to set you free. As you reflect on the following insights, you may want to identify where all of this is packed into the baggage that you are carrying.

The Performance Trap (Addiction): God's answer is justification (Romans 5:1)

Demanding too much of themselves, performance addicts believe they must achieve to secure love. Those who suffer from it believe that performing better, perfecting appearance and achieving status

---

[51] McGee, Robert. 2003. *The Search for Significance*. Nashville: Thomas Nelson

will secure the love and respect of others. They are not focused on what they are doing. They are focused on the outcome of their actions.

Performance addicts are never in the present, they are always thinking of their to-do lists. They turn to activity and busyness like an alcoholic turns to a drink. Unless they're busy, they don't feel worthy. They have trouble listening, slowing down, sleeping, enjoying unstructured time, and poor self-care. Those who suffer from performance addiction must:

- Learn how to listen. Develop your capacity for empathy.

- Slow yourself down. Try always to be in the moment.

- Make self-care a priority – valuing exercise and good nutrition.

- Give your children your love, not your anxiety. Children who have parents with performance addiction may develop it too.

- Stop criticizing the people around you. Performance addicts are always looking for ways to improve themselves, their spouse, and their family.

- Allow yourself to make mistakes without feeling that *you* are a mistake.

Approval Addiction: God's answer is reconciliation (Colossians 1:21-22)

Approval addiction involves people living in bondage to what other people think about them. Criticism of any type makes them feel shamed and small. Approval addicts are people who structure their life around other people's opinion of them – giving other people access to their identity who should not have it. They, in effect, become what others think of them. And, when they are criticized, will strike back with hostility and aggression even if it is constructive.

When the only thing that matters is how I am perceived by my world, I cannot live in God's full acceptance of who I am. And, my deep need for approval will keep me from living in God's love. Because, whatever we are addicted to we are controlled by, our addiction affects and influences every areas of our lives. Approval addiction not only affects our personal relationships, but also our prayer life, how we spend our time, and ultimately whether or not we fulfill our God ordained purpose in the earth.

In her book, *Approval Addiction*, Joyce Myers suggests that insecurity is the root cause of approval addiction. People who are insecure want and need the approval of others so much that they will do just about anything to get it. The truth is, when we are secure, we approve of ourselves, we have confidence, and we accept and love ourselves in a healthy, balanced way. When we are insecure, we disapprove of ourselves, we lack confidence, and we tend to reject ourselves.[52]

The Blame Game: God's answer is propitiation (I John 4:-11)

When something goes wrong and you are never responsible, there is a problem. When someone else is always the culprit, and you are always absolving yourself of responsibility for the issue, again, there is a problem. This is "The Blame Game". In addition to being frustrating and a waste of time, the blame game can also be very counter-productive. By shifting the focus to who made the mistake, which led to the problem, the blame game distracts you from getting at the reason the problem occurred in the first place. As a result you cannot creatively address the problem, and you miss out on a valuable learning experience which could have fostered your growth.

The motivations behind the blame game are centered on the need to be liked and accepted. There is a fear that taking responsibility for an issue will make them disliked, and this could potentially mean rejection and disassociation. Therefore, people who want to look good in the eyes of others are not willing to accept responsibility for any problem so they

---

[52] Myers, Joyce. 2007. *Approval addiction: Overcoming your need to please everyone.* New York: Faith Words

will pass the blame on rather than dealing with it. Others are blamed for their failures, their struggles with society, their lack of success or achievement and their lack of meaningful relationships.

All of us are wrong about something at some point in our lives. The law of averages preclude you from being right all the time. Don't play this game:

- **Don't blame others for your mistakes.** Blaming someone else does not excuse you from responsibility or accountability.

- **When you do feel that someone is genuinely blamable, do so constructively.** It is an opportunity for all to grow in appreciation of each other's gifts and uniqueness.

- **Take ownership for your failures.** A willingness to invest in your failures creates greater self-awareness and as such, facilitates better self-management.

- **Determine to learn from your mistakes.** Every mistake is an opportunity to become more excellent, more accomplished and more accepting of others.

The Shame Trap: God's answer is regeneration (John 3:3-6)

Shame is an unrelenting feeling of not being wanted and of being unworthy of being wanted. Unlike embarrassment, which works among people, shame works within people creating feelings of worthlessness, self-hatred and despair. People who have been shamed dread being caught in a mistake because they believe themselves to be a mistake, labeling themselves as stupid, a failure, or even a burden to others. John Bradshaw, in *Healing the Shame That Binds You*, calls toxic shame 'spiritual bankruptcy'. Shame is toxic and can rob you of spiritual capital – disconnecting you from your identity in Christ. Often the shamed individual will defend themselves against bad feelings by giving the shame away, attacking others, becoming hyper-critical and creating a false sense of superiority to avoid becoming submerged into feelings of inferiority themselves.[53]

    Challenging shame is very difficult. Healing shame is a slow process. The first step is awareness. The shame bound person does not recognize shame is the reason for his or her feelings of worthlessness, because shame exists at the very core of one's being. Therefore, healing from shame involves dealing with the wounds of childhood, grief, and giving voice to one's inner child

    There are a lot of deeply rooted issues and lies that drive and complicate life for most African Americans. Yet the commonality of these universal issues, are compounded even more, by the lies we believe about ourselves beyond race and societal acceptance. These are deeply personal lies that

---

[53] Bradshaw, John. 2005. *Healing the Shame that Binds You*. Deerfield Florida: HCI Publications

target your identity and being. To not acknowledge this as true is to scapegoat the pain, making it society's problem, and never digging deep enough to unearth the schemes of the evil one that are designed to compromise your wellbeing. True growth in the journey is found at the intersection of responsibility and accountability where I affirm those experiences that are uniquely my own that have created pain, distance, and hostility in my life and relationships.

The origin of this kind of pain is rooted in false beliefs: I must meet certain standards in order to feel good about myself; I must be approved by certain others to feel good about myself; those who fail are unworthy of love and deserve to be punished; I am what I am, I cannot change. I am hopeless. These areas, as outlined by McGee must be explored fully. You must identify the lies that you live by. These are specific lies, all based on false beliefs, all exposed by the light of God's love for you.

To begin the process of healing, you must not only recognize the lies you have believed about you, but you must also recognize the specific cultural lies that you have lived by which have also compromised your wellbeing. The psalmist writes,

> He reached down from on high, he took me; he drew me out of mighty waters. He delivered me from my strong enemy and from those who hated me; for they were too mighty for me. He

confronted me in the day of my calamity; but the Lord was my support."

- Psalm 18:16-19

Reflect on this truth. The Lord has been your support bringing you out of many waters of trouble – delivering you from many enemies, of people and systems. Now, ask the Holy Spirit to shed light on the places of darkness where you may have been driven by false beliefs. Ask the Holy Spirit to allow you to see the enemy's schemes, exposing the lies that you have believed. The Lord is your support. His hand is strong upon you as you step into this place of truth.

Chapter Eleven

What Do You See In The Mirror?

We gather information about our identity from the environment that we live and grow in. During our formative years we glean, from the conversations and lessons of our elders and our culture, some sense of who we are. Where we lived and who we interacted with gave birth to the attitudes and assumptions that we have about our identity. If, in our formation, those who raised us questioned their identity as the image of God, or perceived themselves as inferior because of the social constructs of racism, then they would have, for the most part, passed those same dubious feelings along to us.

African Americans range in color from 'charcoal black' to 'high yellow' we range in varying body structures, and in many instances our 'coloring' and 'body structure' assaults the concept of self-image because of larger society's definition of beauty. The question is, if I cannot reconcile my self-image as key to my self-identity, how can I reconcile my self-identity as the "image of God"? To find wholeness as it relates to image, whether self-image, or self as the "image of God", requires that we revisit what has impacted our lives from our earliest formation to the significant experiences that have shaped how we have experienced "the self" as African American Christians.

For many years the larger societal structure denied humanity to African American people, discriminating on the basis of skin color. That created a theological paradox which raises the question about the replacement of the gods of Africa with the God of Christianity. The major proponents of the God of Christianity used westernized theology to justify the perilous plight of suffering that was inflicted upon African Americans. The African American Christian or black theological response was to capitalize on the exodus story as a hermeneutical parallel between the oppressed Israelite community and the oppressed African American community. It was a hermeneutic that affirmed God's liberation of Israel as symbolic of God's liberation of African Americans. Oddly, somewhere in this hermeneutic, is lodged a measure of hope and redemption that in some way offered a lessening of the tension of God as liberator and God as Father who would allow the enslavement of His people.

Identity is a core human question. It is about knowing who I am in the context of the community of humanity of which I am a part. Identity is defined as the adoption of certain personal attitudes, feelings, characteristics, and behaviors. Identity is also association with a larger group of people who share those characteristics. For African Americans, as for all Christians, to know who I am as a son or daughter of

God – who I am in Christ, is a key piece to the identity puzzle. Painfully, for many African Americans there is a duality of the self that is in tension with the idea of being wholly integrated into the society of which I am a part, and the self that is fully embraced as the image of God. For most African Americans, the struggle in either case is indistinguishable. It is not always easy to identify myself as "the image of God" in the context of a culture that historically has not affirmed my being. The affirmation of being is essential to healthy self image and the construction of identity. Grappling with the integration of African Americans into the dominant culture has been, and continues to be a collusion of personal and emotional issues as well as issues of social deconstruction.

African American children will have the difficult task of being integrated and socialized into the mainstream of the dominant American culture. Their minority status alone will earn them painful bruises that come from discrimination and societal devaluing. They will discover what it feels like to live as a subordinate in a society that berates them. While much of what creates societal pain for African Americans is subtle and covert, it is yet intense enough and apparent enough to be recognized for what it is – racism.

It takes real effort to "fit in" especially when acceptance is judged through an historical lens of victimization and oppression. Yet it is precisely the experiences of history that must be reconciled for our true identity to emerge – for the image of God to settle into our consciousness as real. We must make peace with the places in our history that have marred and obscured both, our self-image and the formational basis for the construction of our identity. To be conscious of our rich heritage as a people is the starting point. It links us to each other and affirms the place of our community within the dominant culture as a good place. Our sense of identity and image will find its greatest expression within this intra-cultural context.

The protective function of positive ethnic and racial identities has been well documented. So the importance of identity and belonging as a means of achieving psychological anchorage and acceptance is crucial to how well individuals adjust and are able to navigate the sometimes troubling waters of life. Any distortion in identity creates a conflicted self. Elizabeth Walker's work with African American women, helping them to restructure meaning and cohesion as they moved from a state of self-estrangement and disconnection to faith and a more mature and adequate relationship with self, God, and others, asserts that the key element in this process is grace. God's grace allows for an empathic understanding of struggle, chiefly because, of the confounding experiences of racism and oppression. She asserts that the self structures meaning and cohesion through the processes of grace.[54]

The question then is this, how does one see himself or herself wholly when so much of what you are, even who you are, has been rejected by those with the power to define what is acceptable? Even more conflictful is this reality – you may experience some of the same level of rejection from the place you have counted on for full embrace and acceptance of who you are – your own African American community. This is "reflexive racism" that is driven by the need of some African Americans, as a sub-culture, to emulate the values of the dominant culture as a way of assimilating or fitting in.

Ethnic racism is discrimination rooted in the relationship history of African people of the Diaspora in this country and throughout the world. It is hatred or intolerance of another race or other races. Reflexive racism, on the other hand, is discrimination and differences within groups of people of shared history, race, and cultural experiences. This is often displayed by asserting differences in character and intelligence; a belief that some within the group are inherently superior to others within the same group; and feelings or actions of hatred and bigotry toward a person, or persons, within the same racial group.

It is obvious in such a dynamic that even identity, as an African American, can become a source of tremendous pain. We define ourselves in

---

[54] Walker, Elizabeth. 2002.*Dissertation: A model for pastoral counseling with African American women*. Atlanta: Gammon Theological Seminary

relationship to the other members of the group of which we claim to be a part. When we experience, from those who we are in primary relationship with, internal rejection it creates disconnection and without connectedness we experience depression, personal worthlessness, and social despair.

Anxiety and competition characterizes the search for significance in a life that is not yielded to the Lordship of Jesus Christ. Walker is right. If we are to assist our brothers and sisters to move from self-estrangement and disconnection which prevents them from seeing themselves as God sees them, then we have to assist them to move in the direction of faith and a more mature and adequate relationship with self, God, and others.

Spiritual direction nurtures such awareness, assisting individuals to see themselves through God's eyes. It does not diminish in anyway the significant brokenness that is encountered in life, but it does create a wonderful pathway for healing and restoration. "I must regularly meditate on the truths of Scripture regarding my identity, asking that the Holy Spirit take its reality deep within my soul."[55] Inner-healing prayer is a way of accessing the presence of the Lord, to hear Him speak into the places of brokenness that can lead to depression, a lack of personal worth, social despair and compromised wellbeing.

---

[55] Wardle, Terry. 2004. *Outrageous Love, Transforming Power, p. 37.* Siloam Springs, Arkansas: Leafwood Publishers

Life Application

In his book, *The Decline of African American Theology: From Biblical Faith to Cultural Captivity*, Thabiti M. Anyabwile makes a passionate plea for authentic worship and relationship in the African American tradition. Affirming African American identity as the image of God he writes, "God does not exist – and Jesus did not tabernacle among men, suffer the agony of crucifixion, and was not raised from the grave – to affirm the ethnic sense of identity and self-worth of any single people."[56] His premise is simple, while there are distinctions in African American spirituality forged out of the African American experience in this country – deeply cultural distinctions rooted in slavery, God does not so identify with a people solely because of these distinctions. He identifies with broken humanity – all of whom are "His people". We are His image. We are His people and that alone gets His attention. This is what must be affirmed.

Anthony Hoekema states that man as the image of God is more than just being created in God's likeness. He suggests "first we must always see man in the light of his destiny... as we think about man we must see him not just as he is now but also as he may

---

[56] Anyabwile, Thabiti M. 2007. *The Decline of African American Theology: From Biblical Faith to Cultural Captivity, p. 26.* Downers Grove: Intervarsity Press

someday become"⁵⁷. Hoekema speaks of the image of God in terms of the Bible's teaching that everlasting life is the future for all believers. Therefore we must live with ourselves and each other in light of our future destiny. The confusion erupts from an unclear distinction between God-image and self-image.

Hoekema's perspective about the Christian's identity and the image of God and any resultant distortions are tied to the questions of "self-image". This is the ground of spiritual combat if African Americans are to experience authentic healing. Referring to 'The Fall', he suggests that a two-fold perversion of the self-image occurred: "First, the fall was preceded by an inordinate heightening of man's self-image. Adam and Eve wanted to be higher than God."⁵⁸ In disobeying God's command not to eat of the tree of the knowledge of good and evil, they put themselves above God and took into their own hands the decision of what was right or wrong.

Genesis 3:7 tells us that after the sin was committed, the second perversion occurred. "Awareness of their nakedness meant they now had a sense of shame. They later realized they had done wrong and their self-image began to plummet." Hoekema continues…

---

[57] Hoekema, Anthony. 1994. *Created in God's image, p. 96.* Grand Rapids: William B. Erdman's Publishing
[58] Ibid (p. 104)

The second type of perversion is also consistently found in fallen men: that of an inordinately low self-image. Because a man realizes that he falls short of what he should be, he often tends to look down on himself, despise himself, perhaps even hates himself. [59]

The issues of shame, self-hatred and self-image are areas of defeat in the life of many Christians. Carl Rogers stated, "the central core difficulty in people as I have come to know them is that in the great majority of cases they despise themselves, regard themselves as worthless and unlovable."[60] It is not just an identity issue that African Americans struggle with to find wholeness, rather, at the core of their being is a lack of self-acceptance, and self-love. Out of this place of wounding, self-image is shaped. This is the deeper issue.

Many Christians seem to have "a self-image that is more negative than positive, since when they look at themselves, what is at the center of their field of vision is their continued sinfulness and inadequacy, rather than their newness in Christ."[61] The truth is that one's identity as a Christian has been firmly fixed by Christ's shed blood. Our significance is vested in our identity. Living in a fallen world, when we fall, it mars

---

[59] Op cit. (p. 105)
[60] Rogers, Carl. 1958. *Client Centered Therapy.* P. 17. Constable & Robinson London: Limited Publishing
[61] Hoekema, Op. cit. (p. 107)

perspective on our identity – who we are in Christ. This simply means the self-image is in need of renewal and healing. "An accurate understanding of God's truth is the first step toward discovering our significance."[62] When this occurs, healing begins, identity is reaffirmed and self, as image of God is restored.

Such healing transformation occurs best in a spiritual community that is characterized by grace. This is a forgiving and nonjudgmental community. It is a community that recognizes the ills of fallen humanity in all of its evil. And it is an accepting, affirming and loving community that seeks to delight in one another as an incarnational expression of God's unconditional love.

This is the Christ-centered church which is a collection of sinners who have discovered the powerful good news of the gospel, and who are living in refreshing showers of grace. Grace is curative. It is the healing balm of God's love. Grace is the leverage that sets captives free and allows them to see the reflection of God's image within. It transcends race and people. It is the answer to the ills of culture.

---

[62] McGee, Robert S. 2004. *The Search for Significance.* New York: Thomas Nelson

Chapter Twelve

Let the Church Say Amen

The slave trade to the United States had ended by 1810. This gave rise to the birth of an indigenous and growing native-born population of African Americans. All the various cultures and language groups of African descent blended together. More precisely, cultural traditions, religious practices and uniquely finitive or kinship characteristics were the practices that became increasingly identified as "African American".

With the religious revivalism of the awakening, begun in the late 1700's, religion, specifically Christianity, brought a message of hope and sustenance to the slaves. Though prohibited from attending church outside of their master's view, as they worshipped they were able to adapt many African worship patterns. White clergy preached a message of obedience that the slaves were to live by. Many blacks saw these white churches, in which ministers promoted obedience to one's master as the highest religious ideal, as a mockery of the "true" Christian message of equality and liberation as they knew it. But it was precisely because of this that, back in the slave quarters, African Americans organized their on "invisible institution." Through signals, passwords, and messages, not discernible to whites, they called believers to "hush harbors" where they freely mixed African rhythms, singing, and beliefs with evangelical Christianity.[63] These meetings provided one of the few ways for enslaved African Americans to express and enact their hopes for a better future. But it also became the defining context out of which true community would emerge.

Community, in the sense of inclusion, acceptance and belonging, is the place of gathering that reaches into the life of all its members, meaningfully connecting with the life situations of all its members. It is a place where joys and sorrows are equally shared and celebrated. It is the place of co-humanity, where you are encouraged to have hope because of what God is doing and because of who you are as God's child. And, the convergence of this community in the life of the majority of African Americans is found most identifiably in one's church. The church has always been the connecting link. African American life centered around the church even though each had their own families. It was the gathering together of all families that gave support to and assisted each other in coping with the rigors of life.

The church was regarded as the emotional staple of the community. In the church, God meets everyone equally. The church is the hub of the culture

---

[63] Maffly-Kipp "Redeeming Southern Memory: The Negro Race History," in W. Fitzhugh Brundage, ed., *Where Those Memories Grow: History, Memory, and Southern Identity* (UNC Press, 2000), pp. 169-189

and the greatest source of healing and help for the troubling circumstances of black life. The church was symbolic of what it meant to be "in" community. However, while still of the utmost significance, within recent years there seems to be a declining emphasis of church in the life of the African American community.

In February 2010 when Dr. Eddie Glaude, Jr. wrote in the Huffington Post Religion section "the black church is dead," it sparked controversy and conversation throughout the nation. Glaude is Professor of Religion and Chair of the Center for African American Studies at Princeton University. I get his point...

> *Black churches and preachers must find their prophetic voices in this momentous present. And in doing so, black churches will rise again and insist that we all assert ourselves on the national stage not as sycophants to a glorious past, but as witnesses to the ongoing revelation of God's love in the here and now as we work on behalf of those who suffer most.*[64]

Historically the black church has been the heart, and the soul of the black community. It has been a source of inspiration, challenge and change in the culture. It has supplied the voice and the language that has fostered the ongoing reconciliation of slavery

---

[64]Glaude, Eddie. 02/24/2010. Huffington Post Religion. www.huffingtonpost.com/eddie-glaude-jr-phd/the-black-church-is-dead_b_473815.html

as a justice issue in this country. However, many, such as Glaude, believe that a secularization of the black church has diminished its interest in the social and political issues that affect most black people. There are those who attribute the influence of the mega-church phenomena and the "prosperity gospel" as a betrayal of the church's legacy of sacrifice and social justice; believing instead that there is more of a focus on the personal gain of the clergy.

There is also the issue of the "upwardly mobile blacks who perceive assimilation as a signature of success. Many of these blacks are prone to attend traditionally white churches while others will attend mega-churches with a large African American constituency, but led by white pastors. Then, there is the argument that Glaude raises…

> *black churches are – I like houses of worship in other communities – increasingly just another facet of people's lives rather than the central organizing principle: "I am not suggesting that black communities have become wholly secular; just that black religious institutions and beliefs stand alongside a number of other vibrant non-religious institutions and beliefs.*[65]

The black church has a responsibility to the culture. It cannot simply be 'just another religious institution', its role in African American life is too important! As an interpreter of the culture, the church's voice must be heard.

---

[65] Op. cit.

Culture, is a combination of common heritage, beliefs, values, and rituals that are an important aspect of racial and ethnic communities. African Americans are a resilient people who have withstood enslavement and discrimination to lead productive lives. The church has been the encouragement and the bastion of hope that engendered this resilience and subsequently, produced the Civil Rights Movement. It was the shared faith and common experiences of African American people that produced the strongest, most enduring links to each other and that in turn, produced change in the culture.

While I believe there are some merits to the argument that the black church's impact on the black community and in culture has diminished to some degree. In fact, there are some instances in which the church has perpetuated the pain inflicted upon African Americans by society. This is realized most clearly in examining the issue of inclusivity and the larger church's treatment of women.

The church is to be a place and an agent of healing. I am poised towards the church's prophetic role in the holistic health of the African American community. It can be just that, despite the contingencies and arguments raised by Glaude and others. A resurgence of the church's influence can be realized when pastors focus on the church's witness to wholeness of the person, not just salvaging the church as institution. "We've Come This Far By Faith, Leaning on the Lord" is still a relevant anthem of the black church. It resonates deeply within me that the church is the only agency of the black community that is always on our side and that is perfectly position for the healing of souls.

According to a 2007 survey black Americans "are markedly more religious on a variety of measures than the U.S. population as a whole." It cited that 87% of blacks are affiliated with a religion. It also found that 79% of blacks say that religion is "very important in their life."[66] This is a noteworthy finding. It gives support to the significance of the church as central to black life. As a place of hope for the social and moral conscience of the nation, as a place of healing for a broken people, the church is essential to the life of the faithful.

This is the community where Christ is central, where grace abounds, and where love flows generously and acceptingly to all its members. It has been this sense of community that endowed African Americans with the strength, hope, and fortitude to hold on in the times of tribulation.

No matter the bruising, no matter the inequities in education, employment, or health care, it was and is, the strong social, religious, and family connections, embolden by a firm faith in the God of our fathers that defines the African American community. And it is these same prevailing characteristics of community

---

[66] U.S. Religious Landscape Survey, conducted in 2007 by the Pew Research Center's Forum on Religion & Public Life

that we must draw from to create a pathway for healing. This is the season I believe God is calling the church to enter. Let the church say, Amen.

God of our weary years,
God of our silent tears,
Thou who hast brought us thus far
on the way,
Thou who hast by Thy might,
Led us into the light,
Keep us forever in the path, we pray;
Lest our feet stray from the places, our God,
where we met Thee,
Lest, our hearts drunk with the wine of the world,
we forget Thee,
Shadowed beneath Thy hand,
May we forever stand
True to our God, true to our native land!

James Weldon Johnson, 1921

Life Application

True healing occurs in community. For most African Americans, the church is synonymous with community. Does the church you attend fill your need for community? Do you feel safe there? Can you be an authentic hurting individual and know that you will be tended, cared for and loved? These are important questions that you must address if you are to find wholeness in Christ.

Historically, one could point to any African American congregation and safely say that is a church that is passionate about its commitment to the centrality of the Gospel as the motivating force for its communal life. The way that the church embraced its members, how it took a stand against injustice and wrong, were hallmarks of its caring and desire to touch the lives of its members in meaningful ways. However, there are some who believe that the black church has lost that quality of caring. Its relevance and authenticity as a healing community has been compromised by its assimilation and integration efforts to look like main stream churches.

In its effort to portray itself as more sophisticated, and more technologically savvy, there are those who say the black church has ceased being a transformative spiritual community. Conforming to a societal standard that has diluted its prophetic voice and its missional in-reach and outreach, it no longer resembles "the beloved community." It, for the most part, has entered a collusion of deception, where it touts a message of theological soundness, but in practice it hurts people. It does not touch the brokenness of the people, nor does it promote a ministry that promotes gospel intentionality in the world, where individuals are encouraged to really live out the tenets of the gospel in the Christian life. But it should.

In *Exposing the Myth that Christians Should Not Have Emotional Problems*, Dwight Carlson echoes a statement by a psychologist who had just returned from an overseas mission's trip, "The only army that shoots its wounded is the Christian army," said the speaker. He summed up the philosophy of the group he worked with as:

1. We don't have emotional problems. If any emotional difficulties appear to arise, simply deny having them.

2. If we fail to achieve this first ideal and can't ignore a problem, strive to keep it from family members and never breathe a word of it outside the family.

3. If both of the first two steps fail, still don't seek professional help. [67]

---

[67] Carlson, Dwight. *Exposing the Myth that Christians Should Not Have Emotional Problems*. Christianity Today. February 9, 1998

Sadly, there are many churches that hold the attitude that emotional problems are a direct result of personal sin. Surely at the root of most dysfunctional behavior there is the commission of some sin. But the fact that at any given moment, approximately 15 percent of our population is experiencing significant emotional problems suggests that our churches need to be sanctuaries of healing, not places where people must hide their wounds.[68]

In a very real sense the answer to every human problem, whether a broken leg or a burdened heart, is to be found in the redeeming work of Christ on the cross. The issue is not whether our problem is physical, emotional, or spiritual. All problems are spiritual at some level. But is the church the healing community where I can bring my brokenness to the table of the Lord and find healing. Is the community willing to appropriate the spiritual counsel, support and caring that looks like Jesus' kind of caring so that I can be loved into wholeness while I am on my journey to being healed.

The fact that many churches are reluctant to pray for emotionally wounded and broken individuals is a cause for deep concern. Is this really a healing community? I cannot be content at the altar where it is perfectly acceptable to pray for cancer, pneumonia, heart problems and diabetes, but it is not acceptable to affirm and pray for my brokenness and emotional

---

[68] Carlson, Dwight L. *Why Do Christians Shoot Their Wounded.* Downers Grove:IVP

pain; for my friend's bi-polar disorder, a sister's depression or a brother's panic attacks.

*****

By the way, it is important to note that I believe in the healing power of the church as community. It is the frontline of intervention for wounded individuals, and I believe that most people will benefit from spiritual counseling, and the support that comes from the community. I do not want to suggest that is all there is to healing. Issues of salvation, forgiveness, morality, and some domestic issues can all be addressed well with spiritual counseling or formational prayer. A brother or sister who will come alongside of you to hold you accountable for your healing is wonderful. But do not overlook the possibility that some emotional difficulties require professional help. If you, as an individual, or as a person who tends a hurting individual recognize patterns and behaviors of a debilitating and destructive nature that persists, it is a sign that something more is needed.

I believe it is the will of God that all are healed, but I also believe that for many that healing will be ongoing – we are being healed. Our sufficiency must be in Christ, and we access healing through our "one another" relationships. That is what true community is all about. But be wise enough to recognize when you should seek out help!

Chapter Thirteen

How Did We Get Here?
Healing is not supposed to hurt

It is a real epiphany when you realize where you are in your present relationships. It is a journey that did not just begin and your present place of awareness has been in the making for a long time. There have been many alerts, many signs, that there are unsettled places in your life that God wants access to. Few individuals awaken soon enough to the reality that much of the dysfunction, dissatisfaction and disappointment that are experienced in their life and relationships are engineered and driven by unresolved, painful and wounding experiences. When the light does come on, the fallout is great and two questions standout front and center: How did I get here and who can help me?

The question of how I got here is an important one. It requires digging deeply and owning some realities that you most often do not want to revisit. But the good thing is the awareness that you are at a place where help is needed to unravel the knots.

While there are many external, systemic, and societal issues that thwart the lives of African

American individuals, so too are African Americans plagued with the same internal "cause and effect" relationships that create pain for all of God's sons and daughters. When your soul is in pain, it does not sift through your maze of experiences to determine whether the cause of your pain is from external circumstances or internal dissonance. You are simply in pain and though unique to every individual, pain is a universal gift. For all people, the pain that comes from brokenness and human suffering cannot be ignored. It therefore becomes every individual's challenge to take the "stuff" of one's life and allow God to transform it for His use.

Sustained pain from hurt, injury, loss, spiritual disconnectedness, oppression and bondage creates protracted discomfort physically, spiritually and emotionally. But, as a conduit and agent of God's grace, a caregiver can enter into another's suffering and pain to announce God's healing and transformative power. This is the good news, there is no suffering, no pain that God can not heal – nothing that the Holy Spirit cannot touch – no vastness or deepness that God's grace cannot reach. God can redeem all pain, for there is nothing outside the boundaries of God's love and God's forgiveness.

This is the message that I have been sharing with Derek and Pat a deeply hurting middle class African American professional couple who is experiencing acute marital stress.

Pat is Baptist and actively participates in the life of her church. Derek is Catholic, and while upholding what he describes as "Catholic principles" he is less involved, and less connected to his church than Pat. They both profess a faith in God and a desire to follow the principles of faith as taught by Jesus. As followers of Jesus they feel that their faith should provide an overall umbrella of guidance for their relationship. They are both college graduates in their early thirties and have been married for five years. Although Pat wants children, they have no children. They are both engaged in their professional careers. Derek says that he wants children, but he believes there is "too much stuff" going on between them to even talk about children. Their five year marriage has been fraught with ongoing problems that mask the depth of the insecurities, self esteem and trust issues that have each of them in perpetual pain.

Pat reports that there was a lot of pain in her life while growing up. She was close to her three siblings. Although she was the youngest, she felt that her older siblings maintained a heavy dependence on her for emotional, moral and financial support. Her parent's unstable relationship ended in divorce. She never felt connected to her mother – her older sister was more of a mother to her.

Derek reports there was disconnectedness in his family growing up as well. His parents, particularly his father, made rigid demands of him and his two younger siblings. His father was not a warm, loving man, but a strict disciplinarian who only showed any form of acceptance or love when rules were followed. His father died just as Derek entered middle school. His mother remarried. His step father was quite a bit like his natural father. He never felt accepted by him and therefore felt no attachment or closeness to his stepfather. In fact, he felt little attachment to anyone in his family other than his mother.

It was apparent, from our time together, that much of what plagued this marriage stemmed from unresolved issues, brokenness and pain in their families of origin. This was compounded by the fact that they both had been in past relationships that were unfulfilling and that had ended badly. Pat's was a prior marriage and Derek's was a long time cohabitation relationship.

Having experienced pain in their families of origin and subsequently experiencing pain in their past relationships caused them both to view every challenging experience in their marriage as one more disappointment, one more failure of expectations that it was possible to find happiness and contentment with anyone. The more they viewed each other through such a lens, the more emotional distance it created between them holding them hostage to a plethora of presuppositions, premature and false conclusions that reinforced their relationship pain.

While it was clear that Derek and Pat really loved each other, they had concluded that because of their marital problems they should probably live apart and not move forward with their plans to purchase a new home. Because of their problems, they doubted the future of their marriage. This decision to live apart was to be, in effect, a temporary separation to allow each of them to gain perspective on their future.

A few weeks into their separation, Pat discovered that Derek's involvement with a mutual friend, Lisa, had become more and more frequent. In short, Pat discovered that Derek had been involved in an extramarital affair with Lisa. Pat found out about the affair accidentally. She was visiting Derek's apartment when she discovered romantic greeting cards and female clothing items that were not hers.

In approaching Derek about these discoveries, his defensiveness and aversive behavior was an indication that something was wrong. After what Pat describes as a "huge blow-up" Derek admitted to the affair and that he had been involved with Lisa for a while. In this confrontation Derek also told Pat that he was no longer certain if he loved her – they have "irreconcilable" differences and so much ongoing drama they should just dissolve their marriage. Pat was devastated by this new information and thus began her spiral into a deeper well of more pain and suffering.

After some days had passed, Derek attempted to talk through where they were as a result of this new information. He also stated that at some level he still wanted a relationship with Pat, but he did not want the pain. He informed her that he had visited the priest of the local Catholic Church that he occasionally attended. In approaching the priest about ending his marriage, the priest had tapped into some places of brokenness in Derek's life that actually had very little to do with his marriage, rather, because he had placed so much hope in the fulfillment that he thought marriage would bring, whenever he was disappointed it moved quickly to devastation, to his feeling that no one (Pat in this case) really understood him or cared about him.

The priest suggested Derek and Pat should meet with someone to talk about the stresses that were making their marriage so painful. Pat was uncomfortable with going to her pastor because she wasn't sure how he would react to such a "prominent couple" being in such a bad place. She also wasn't comfortable with going to the priest because she felt he, not being married, could not possibly understand her side of the story. Yet, feeling like they had each messed up so much of their lives already, they agreed to counseling as a part of the process to help them to determine if they could have a future together. Through a later conversation with the parish priest, a referral was made to me for marriage counseling.

Early on, in our initial meetings, the depth of their pain was obvious. The first thing that was very clear is neither of them had ever really told anyone their story – that alone heightened their pain. They each felt misunderstood, and in every give and take, no matter what was discussed it always became personal. Somehow they only heard the message of how deficient they each were and how unlikely either of them could ever be anything but a further source of pain for each other. What they had never discovered is they were each responding to the other from a place of pain deep within themselves that actually had little to do with their marriage. Their history of disappointment and feelings of being misunderstood were triggered every time one told the other that they didn't measure up in some way. I sensed it was important to unearth what had been deeply buried. The fruit from the seeds sown in that painful soil was destructive. Without help it was doubtful that they could live into a better pattern – one that could be life giving and life affirming.

Life Application

No one ever wakes up and says, "I have decided to be in pain, and because I am in such pain, I am committed to making you hurt also. Therefore, every word I say, every action, and with every opportunity that presents itself, as much as it is possible with me, I assure you that we are going to swim in a deep sea of pain, and that's just that!" No, it doesn't happen that way, but when you are there, it certainly feels like it. That's what it felt like to Pat and Derek.

You have encountered your own painful places. Perhaps you have not honored those places, even tried to escape them, or blame them on someone else. But as we continue to look at what happens in the life of this couple, Pat and Derek, see yourself in their story and take the risk to enter in.

Work begins at the place of pain – an acknowledgment that "I am hurting, but I don't want to". After working through blame and after covering some necessary steps with them, I was able to get Pat and Derek to rediscover that they did not set out one day to find a victim to inflict this unbearable emotional pain upon. They gradually got there, and in that journey, they had indeed believed some significant lies which were driving their lives

In the marriage counseling sessions I chose the path of discovery with them. By this I mean we needed to uncover the plots, stories and themes of their relationship. It was vitally important to discover the root sources of their pain as individuals and as a couple, before we could move to a place of liberating truth. In truth, they could begin to see that God wanted them to live into a larger story – their story could indeed line up with His story for them. But it would require healing.

It became clearer and clearer that Pat was in the greater pain. While Derek too was in pain, he seemed less anxious and less incapacitated by their current situation. There was an overall sense of resignation with him that caused me to wonder if he would be open to really trusting God in this hard place. A part of him was ready to "let go". For Pat, this was not the case. She was, "believing God for her marriage". She adulates, loves and adores Derek. In her words…"I had him on a pedestal, he could do no wrong. I made him my life and now he has robbed me of my life. I am devastated by this, not just the affair but the fact that I have lived a lie with him for five years."

In Pat's mind Derek was a perfect person – he could do no wrong. She admits that there were lots of arguments and senseless fighting. She also reports that their intimacy had declined with little to no sexual relationship between them for the past seven months. But she never imagined that Derek did not love her or that he would be unfaithful to their marriage vows. "What's wrong with me", she said through a flood of tearful emotion, "am I not worthy of being loved by anyone?" It was at this point that my focus changed from the acute anxiety of the marriage breakdown to the acute dissonance resulting from blame low self esteem that Pat was experiencing – the greater source of her pain. This is where her healing had to begin.

I asked Derek's permission to bracket the issues of infidelity and divorce temporarily to allow me some time with Pat. To my amazement he readily agreed to this suggesting that he would like to have the same opportunity to unpack some things himself. With his permission and support I began formational counseling with Pat.

Pat initially blamed herself for Derek's indiscretion. Because she always saw him as such a good person, she was convinced that there was something defective about her that gave birth to all that she was going through. She felt that God was punishing her because she had not tried hard enough to please Derek and to get beyond her insecurities and low self esteem. When asked where she had gotten this information that she was being punished for not being the perfect wife, she described years of hurtful putdowns stemming from her family of origin. There were so many cut offs, so much lack of validation and affirmation at significant places in her life's journey. As she looked at the picture she had painted of her family of origin and early life experiences (I used the genogram as a primary tool for this discovery) she realized that there had been little affirmation, love and acceptance from her family. With no shared closeness and no one to ever celebrate her she was not sure what validation, or affirmation from Derek even looked like. In fact, steady on a course of pleasing him, of all the experiences over the past five years with Derek she had been made to feel ingratiated, and unworthy of "such a good person". She lost herself in the process.

We were now at the point where Pat was able to acknowledge that it was not her fault that she had experienced such difficult places in her life. With a harsh, judging father who had little to do with her after the divorce, and a detached mother, she never felt welcome, belonging or delight. The closest she got to that was the care and attention she received from her oldest sister, who was maternalistic towards her, and who also made unhealthy and unreasonable demands of her, riddling her with guilt – shaming her, when she did not measure up. The end result, she learned to get acceptance by people pleasing and self-ingratiation. When she did not please, love and affection were withheld as punishment. Pat was the victim of core woundings that had ripped her identity away from her early in life. She could neither see herself as loveable, nor capable of doing anything that would ever score her enough points to be worthy.

After hearing the truth of the Lord's great love for her – reassuring her of her incredible value and worth to him – regardless of the messages she had told herself all these years, Pat was ready to start movement towards freedom. In the process of caring for Pat, she began to experience significant healing for the deep wounds that informed the lens through which she viewed her life. She became hope-filled and delightfully overwhelmed by the reality of God's non-judgmental love for her. It was as if she had never heard this message before. Maybe she had, but now it sunk deep into the core of her being.

Guiding her into the presence of the Lord, helping her to find a place of safety for recalling the losses of her life – she was able to begin to grieve. In her journey of inner healing, she is now able to hear the truth, God lavishly loves her, and He is inviting her into a wonderful life.

By the way, while it seems that Derek has been left out – or off the hook, not to worry, the changes and freshness with which Pat has begun to approach her life has created such interest in Derek, that he has become exceptionally open, receptive and welcoming towards her. And that is often the case, lessening her defenses and allowing herself to feel loved lessened his resistance and defenses. He is working on his issue and experiencing the wonder of God's love in a new way too.

If you are to grow in the journey of healing, there are some things that have to be settled. First you have to affirm that it is your journey. This simply means that it will matter to you much more than it will matter to anyone else. In fact, much of what you will encounter will be so intensely personal that it may appear that no one else is interested in where you are heading. You have to be ok with that. This means that you have to be open to the internal issues that impact your life, as well as the external ones. For most African Americans, the internal issues gathered around relationships are very much the same as they are for all people. The difference for us is that many times the external issues, chiefly those rooted in racism and social rejection, will often intensify the internal issues as we seek to make sense of our story.

Secondly, you must become comfortable with God's confrontation. God is not going to enter into this process with you to give support to where you already are. He enters because he wants you to arrive at a better place. He is calling you to that. You may have no idea of where that place is in the moment. But each moment is an unfolding of where God is leading. If you are deliberate and intentional about following, there will be clear signs along the path. They will not be shrouded in mystery, but gilded with a sense of 'this is God's doing'. And so, it means that some of what God calls forth may stretch you to uncomfortable places and uncomfortable choices, but always to a wider reality of your preciousness.

Thirdly, when you come to a crossroad and ask yourself those two questions: how did I get here? And, is there anyone who can help me? Don't be afraid to seek a guide – a person who can be co-human with you who is capable of helping you navigate the troubling waters that have upset your soul. There is nothing wrong with getting help!

Fourthly, you must expect God to show up – to be there, in the journey with you – no one else, just the Holy Spirit who can lead you to the deepest places of truth. There will be other travelers, but they will be on their own journey and even when He brings a guide along the path for you, it is for clarity, for comforting companionship and spiritual direction, so that you will know that you are not alone.

Finally, you must recognize the resting places in the journey. There are resting places. These are places of celebration, places of victory, and awakenings in the soul that call you to "Sabbath" celebration. A day, a week, a year, a season, rest in these places, awaiting renewed strength and life for the journey ahead.

Chapter Fourteen

The Source of Truth

Jesus said, "I am the way, and the truth, and the life. No one comes to the Father but through me". John 14:6

Of the many miracles that Christ performed in the gospels, the most dramatic were healing miracles. By his touch, the lame walked, the blind received sight, and some who had been infirmed for years were healed. A lot of attention is given to these physical manifestations of Christ's power to heal. But Jesus also performed healings of the mind – emotional healings. There are numerous instances in the gospels of Matthew, Mark, and Luke, where He cast out demons from those who were possessed. And in each instance, they were restored to wholeness in body, soul, and spirit. The apostle Paul echoed that mandate, "And the very God of peace sanctify you wholly; and I pray God your whole spirit and soul and body be preserved blameless unto the coming of our Lord Jesus Christ" (1 Thessalonians 5:23).

Jesus also commissioned His disciples to be agents of His healing grace. As the Truth, and the source of truth, He commissions us still to embrace the healing mandate because He desires your wholeness. The Hebrew word for heal is *"rapha"*, which means to make thoroughly whole. The Greek word *"sozo"* has the same connotation. It is used inter-changeably throughout the Greek New Testament to mean to "save" and to "heal". Therefore, to be whole is to be free of "...the sin which doth so easily beset us..." (Hebrews 12:1).

Whether sickness in your body, anxieties and fears that assail your mind or fears lodged in your soul, God wants you thoroughly washed, cleansed – He wants you to be made whole. This process of cleansing is about your sanctification. It is the same process of cleansing and healing that Jeremiah pronounces to Israel, "Nevertheless I will bring health and healing to it; I will heal my people and will let them enjoy abundant peace and security" (Jeremiah 33:5).

John 14:6 is often quoted as the singular text to declare Jesus as the Truth and the only source of truth. I often wonder if we really understand the significance and power of such a statement. If Jesus is the truth, and the source of truth, meaning the only real thing, then why is life marred and weighed down with so many substitutes, and false truths?

Part of what this verse teaches is that we cannot know the fullness of truth until we come to terms with the Truth – Jesus Christ as the only way a person can be reconciled to God. It is as if the soul is longing for its reunion with God, the Father as it was in the beginning. If reconciliation, in this respect, means I can only enter into a life of truth through Jesus Christ, then all of a sudden, this text makes a lot of sense. The source of truth is what I must be reconciled to. Even saying this suggests the possibility that I have lived outside of truth, and to some degree have embraced a false truth.

Three dynamics are helpful to understanding what this means: Jesus as the "Way", Jesus as the "Truth", and Jesus as the "Life".

Jesus as The Way

A way is a path or route. When the disciples had expressed some confusion about where Jesus was leading them, he simply reminded them, "follow me". We hear that command in the words "I am the way" – meaning the only way – path or route to your salvation or wholeness. It is important that I come to terms with this reality. I cannot find wholeness outside of Christ. I can only find true union with God, the Father, through the Son, Jesus Christ. Many people spend an inordinate amount of life, time, and energy trying to get around this. In his *Confessions,* the African Bishop, St Augustine said it best: "God, you have made us for yourself, and our hearts are restless till they find their rest in you."

If I find ultimate rest in the one who made me for himself then there is a God-shaped hole inside of me that only God can fill. To even attempt to fill that space with anything else is a lie, it is not the truth, it is a substitute. Cars, gadgets, toys can't fill it. Flat screen televisions are wonderfully distracting and entertaining, but when the show is over, the hole is still in your soul. Simply put, things can not fill the hole in your soul that is uniquely shaped for God. Out of all our yearnings, it is not more of this or that, that will satisfy, only the one who is the truth can free us to allow God to fill us.

The insatiable hunger for more, the nagging edge that lingers, reminding us of unfulfilled hopes and dreams, all reflecting just how broken we really are, is the heart's quest for truth. It is the quest for what will truly satisfy.

Many African Americans seek fulfillment through personal ambition and accomplishments, arriving at a plateau of success only to discover that they are still on edge. It's as if you are almost there, but not quite. Much of the edginess stems from unresolved issues of pain that have been denied, discounted or purely ignored. But the truth is, the realities of what you had to go through to get to where you got to, is lodged into the recesses of your being as an unavoidable reality holding you in bondage to multi-layers of lies and substitutes. Avoidances that you have refused to look at or acknowledge will always eclipse the significance of your seeming successfulness.

Jesus as The Truth

Truth has to do with authority and law. Jesus, as the incarnate Word of God is the Truth and he is the source of all truth. Jesus is the Truth, and our ultimate fulfillment is found in the Truth. He is the revelation of God, the Word of God made flesh referred to as 'truth' in the Gospel of John – the gospel of life, more than 22 times. Why is this so important? It is important because we are made for God – to glorify him and to reflect his glory in our relationships with one another. Sure, there are many relationships that may have been the source of intractable pain, but living in such relationships without the truth is a setup for more pain and brokenness. Like the Psalmist, we make the discovery that there is a yearning in the soul to connect with the Truth, "my soul is yearning for you, my God" (Psalm 42:1). And as the psalmist reminds us, in our most salient moments we must acknowledge that God alone satisfies. He alone fills the emptiness of our lives, "O God, you are my God, for you I long" (Psalm 63:1).

Jesus as The Life

Jesus told His disciples about his impending death but he also told him that he would rise again. In declaring, "I lay down my life for my sheep and I take it up again" (John 10:13). In establishing his authority over life and death, he was demonstrating that there is no adversary that can capture or hold those who live for and trust in him.

When this truth is understood, the church is empowered to live out His life, as the "called out" ones. Yet, the church has always been in tension with the truth, particularly as truth relates to how the church is to serve people's lives. Sometimes, misguided and missing its purpose, the church fails to focus "The Life" which reflects Jesus' ultimate concern for people. Without this awareness as the primary pillar upon which the church becomes a healing community, it will forget that truth is not a product of social construction, but is grounded in the authenticity of scripture and confidence in the promises of Jesus. The heart of the Gospel rests in this awareness and the fact that in love, for His creation, Jesus willingly chose to redeem humanity's brokenness by dying on the cross. In his death, we were freed from the dominion of sin and Satan. And in his death and resurrection he secured for us a restored relationship with God that brings pardon and peace, acceptance and access, and adoption into God's family (Colossians 1:20, 2:13-14; Romans 5:1-2; Galatians 4:4-7; 1 Peter. 3:18).

Life Application

It is at the intersection of what God has done in Christ Jesus, and what we have done in acts of unrighteousness, that we now understand the ministry of reconciliation. In our brokenness, we have been hurt, and we have hurt others. On the surface we may make an attempt to justify the pain that we have caused, based on the fact that we ourselves were hurt.

It is as simple as acknowledging that the sins committed against us as an African American people have been grievous and wrong, but there are also sins that we have committed that have been, in many instances, equally hurtful against one another and against those who have hurt us. In embracing the Truth we are able to see our culpability and insensitivity. We are able to see that we need a healthy dose of truth to find freedom from the weights of sin that hold us captive. Once free we can live a more Christ filled, godly life. We need to embrace the truth with the confidence of John 8:32, "whoever the Son sets free, is free indeed." There is no other solution.

To hold someone accountable for the pain that they have caused me is to ignore the pain that I have caused someone. Such compromise is a twisting of truth that is better understood as sin. So it is that as I realize my need for more and more of Christ, I am humbled, turning in repentance to those whom I have hurt, to be more of Christ for them – that is reconciliation.

It is not a minimizing or dismissing of my pain. Rather it is to acknowledge the one who took on the pain of us all, that we may now turn in love and forgiveness towards others. We have one life, and in our journey towards Christ-likeness, we hold tenaciously to the one who is the Truth. As we do this, we trust Him for the healing that we need; for the ability to be reconciled to those who caused our pain and to live in a place of greater understanding of who I am – my identity in Christ – giving Him full reign in my life.

In the case of Pat and Derek, truth meant to reacquaint them with God's love. It also required explaining to Pat that there are places in our lives where we must step up to the plate, so to speak, and take responsibility for turning our lives around—for making small or big changes that will make our lives and the lives of those we love better. This is cooperating with the truth. For Pat, that meant taking more responsibility for her own happiness, not only affirming the wonder of who she is as God's daughter, but also to affirm her right to be devastated, angry and hurt. There is room for such discovery in God's love.

Getting a glimpse of how God sees her, she no longer wallows in self pity, believing she is not "good enough" for Derek, but rather she has begun the process of disputing the lies and distortions – the enemy's attacks on her identity, and she can now hear the truth of who she is: loved (1John 3:3), accepted (Ephesians 1:6), child of God (John 1:12), redeemed and forgiven (Colossians 1:14),complete in Christ (Colossians 2:10, free from condemnation (Romans 8:1), and many more wonderful truths that are ushering new freedom into her life. For Derek it meant accepting responsibility for his indiscretions and working towards rebuilding trust and forgiveness in their relationship.

Admittedly, I wanted to "fix" what was broken with Pat and Derek. That was the Holy Spirit's job. To cooperate with what the Holy Spirit was doing, it was my job to help them to see where He was moving. They each needed to go deeper into the truth in order for them to gain that awareness. Doing so, they realized that their journey did not begin overnight, neither would it end overnight. Their journey was an accumulation of years of unresolved pain and hurtful experiences that caused deep emotional fall out. If I can be the resonating voice of God's presence and power in helping them to struggle with the hard places in their journey, in time I believe they both will be able to speak truth to the lies and false beliefs that have driven so much of their relationship. They will come to realize that God would not allow their pain and suffering unless He could draw a greater good out of it – that He is the Way, the Truth, and the Life so desperately needed to bring them to a place of wholeness and well-being.

Where is God in your pain? As a pastor and clinical counselor I have discovered that people do not want a pedestal or idol, they want someone who is co-human – someone who feels as they feel, to help them navigate the maize of ambiguities, complexities and pitfalls erupting from their brokenness. In formational prayer, I am co-human. For it is only to the degree that I have found freedom through the Truth that I can be that real person who can articulate the healing grace of God for Pat and Derek. Suffering is a stage in the spiritual life.

To pretend to inoculate yourself, or to pretend that you will not encounter hurtful experiences that can create pain is to deceive oneself and to adopt a reductionist view of God. Simply, the character and flavor of that which causes one's pain is uniquely related to God's plan and purpose for one's life. This is Job's story and it has to be our story too if we are to grow in the journey. If we believe God is just, when we chose to live in the truth, and allow God's grace to touch our humanness, growth and healing can take place. Romans 8:28 is the ultimate truth of this reality. "We are assured and know that [God being a partner in their labor] all things work together and are [fitting into a plan] for good to and for those who love God and are called according to [His] design and purpose" (Amplified).

Who has hurt me? Who have I hurt? These are two crucial questions, when answered, propels me towards living into greater awareness of the truth. It is often easy to survey one's life and identify the places and landings that left us emotionally scarred and jaded. And we accentuate the impact of profound despair inflicted upon us from those places and landings that contain any measure of injustice or discrimination.

We have been hurt, but we have also hurt. The fact that one's pain may have resulted from ethnic disparity, parental inversion, abandonment, or another's pain may have resulted from situational circumstances or even sibling disputing only makes real the truth that each of us have the propensity to create pain for another. To allow the Lord to meet me in the places of my pain is to affirm this truth and seek the healing that is available to me. From a place of wholeness I may also be restored in relationship to those who have hurt me, and those whom I have hurt. This is the truth that flows from an authentic love of Jesus Christ.

Chapter Fifteen

Why Must I Forgive – Can't I Just Say I'm Sorry?

"When you hold resentment toward another, you are bound to that person or condition by an emotional link that is stronger than steel. Forgiveness is the only way to dissolve that link and get free." – Catherine Ponder

May 2007 was an exciting time for Sharon and me. This was the month and year we became grandparents. Officially marking our arrival to the next stage of life, it was now, not hard to imagine, for all of us, our days are numbered and we must do our best to make every day count – especially for those we love.

Becoming grandparents is really a significant and delightful life passage. There are joys to be anticipated, new adjustments to be made, as you decide on what this little one will call you. We chose "Papa" for me and "Noni" for Sharon. There are also the negotiations that come with preparing our home for our new grandbaby's arrival, as well as figuring out where we will fit in with our new baby's care. It was important to us that we assisted our son and daughter-in-law in making our first grandchild's advent into the world the most glorious and celebrated event of our lives.

In the momentary reflecting on where we are on the continuum of life, we were completely overtaken by the awe of this premature little one, born two and a half months too soon. She was a "preemie" in every sense of the word. She could be held in the palm of her daddy's hand – so tiny. But, there was a fierce spark of life in her. The signs were there early on that she intended to be here and if she had her way about it that is exactly what it would be. Janae Nicole Siler had her way about it. She is here, strong in body, strong in spirit, hugely bright, and a real keeper. She has captured our hearts, and she knows it.

Now a few years older, I cannot resist when she says "Papa let's dance ." She has yet to figure out that I have two left feet, but we twirl, bend, bow and dip as if we are dancing with the stars – what fun, what hilarity!

This day, Janae is not very happy with her Papa. She had her first lesson in the necessary art of forgiveness. She had decided it was ok to playfully kick and hit. But when I corrected her, she did not understand this was not acceptable behavior. After trying to cajole her into an apology of sorts, anything to make me think she kind of half way got it, that's when it happened. She kicked me – not once, but twice. Me – her Papa! That's when the lesson began. I disciplined her in the way that all good papas do – two swats on the backside. Of course the injury was of rescue squad proportions – such wailing as you have never heard. After the storm had subsided, we talked about why she cannot hit or kick others, even if she is unhappy with them! I explained why this was not a good thing, not even to be done in jest!

Thinking I had made the necessary amends so that we could re-enter our wonderful world of love for each other, I asked her for an apology and here is where the lesson really began. With a prompt folding of the arms, a quick right gyration of her little body, and a flip of her head away from me, she said with as much remorse and enthusiasm as the Grinch that stole Christmas, S O R R Y! In that moment, I saw the fight of the preemie that was determined that she was going to be here – a spirit that I would admire under most circumstances. But my little Janae had a lesson to learn today. At three years old, she had to learn the lesson of forgiveness, a genuine "I am sorry" that pleadingly asks, please forgive me and accept me. Please allow me to make amends so that we can re-enter our cherished world.

It was a long day for me and Janae, but I was counting on the fact that she cherished our world as much as I and that she indeed wanted to re-enter. Some moments later, pride abandoned, and love remembered, uncoerced, I heard, "I'm sorry papa." I melted. I swooped her up, hugged her tightly, kissed her tenderly. We resumed our dance, what fun, what hilarity – all was forgiven, we were restored. Our world was safe again.

The lesson of forgiveness is hard for all of us, not just babies born prematurely. While we could not wait to provide unconditional love, kindness, patience, humor, comfort and all the goodies, and other things her parents would say she could not have, (that grandparents always think are okay), there was a lesson that had to be learned. A precursory "sorry" is not an authentic apology, nor is it a remedy for needed forgiveness for a wrong done.

I love the way my son, Jonathan, and his wife, Andrea parent our granddaughter. Andrea has a loving touch, Jonathan is a bit firmer, but they both have a gentle nature with their daughter. Janae is blessed to be born into a happy and stable marriage and a God-centered home with lots of people to lavish love on her. But she still had to learn, and will continue to learn, the powerful lessons of forgiveness and the difficulty in according the same when she feels violated or wronged by someone. It is a lesson that has to be learned simply because forgiveness indeed is the key to allowing us to enter and re-enter our cherished world, fully embraced, unconditionally and lovingly restored when acceptance is needed and wanted.

Forgiveness is important for healing. We all have to deal with hurt, anger, and the temptation to want to get even. As African Americans we have endured more than our share of wrongs done to us, un-amended wrongs in society, wounds from family, friends, and loved ones who mow over our feelings like cutting grass. Yet, there is a place that we are called to live with one another. It is our cherished world, and when that world is shattered, no matter who the offender is, it hurts and it is so hard to get back to that world. ==Forgiveness is hard work.==

I believe that is why Paul, in his letter to the church in Philippi, wrote: "I count not myself to have apprehended: but this one thing I do, forgetting those things, which are behind, and reaching forth unto those things, which are before" (Philippians 3:13, KJV). Paul was clear that sin is to be acknowledged. Wrong done to us is to be acknowledged, but to be overcome by the willful and deliberate actions of others to hurt us, to be preoccupied with getting even with them places us at risk of greater injury. We may miss what God has for us. Therefore, Paul says, "press toward the mark of the prize of the high calling of God in Christ Jesus" (Philippians 3:14, NKJV). This is good news when you are tempted to hold onto a grudge because of a wrong done to you. God says, keep your eye on me, there is so much more.

Peter asked Jesus how often he was to forgive a "brother" who had sinned against him, and offered up the number "seven" as a possible answer. Jesus responded: "I do not say to you, up to seven times, but up to seventy times seven" (Matthew 18:22,

NKJV). In reference to the result of "seventy times seven", 490 times, John MacArthur writes, "No one can possibly keep count of such a high number of offenses. But that is precisely the point! Keeping count has nothing to do with true forgiveness. If an offense is sincerely forgiven, it cannot be held against the offender." [69]

In Romans 12:19-21 Paul writes:

Do not take revenge, my friends, but leave room for God's wrath, for it is written: "It is mine to avenge; I will repay," says the Lord. On the contrary: "If your enemy is hungry, feed him; if he is thirsty, give him something to drink. In doing this, you will heap burning coals on his head." Do not be overcome by evil, but overcome evil with good.

This scripture teaches us about our responsibility to forgive those who sin against us. However, many individuals are stuck at a place of unforgiveness largely because of the lack of repentance of those who have hurt them.

Romans 12, seems to suggest that we must not only forgive those who offend us, but we must not seek revenge – we can't get even, and on top of that we are to bless our offender. If they are hungry, we must feed them. If they are thirsty, we must give them

---

[69] MacArthur, John. 2009. *The Freedom and Power of Forgiveness*. Wheaton Illinois: Crossway Books

a drink. And, even though doing this "you will heap burning coals on his head" that does not seem to be enough to cool the fire that burns within when someone sins against us.

Some individuals believe you can only forgive those who repent and therefore the unrepentant is not deserving of forgiveness. They use such scriptures as Luke 17:3-4: "*If your brother sins, rebuke him, and if he repents, forgive him. If he sin against you seven times in a day, and seven times comes back to you and says, `I repent,' forgive him.*" The intent of this scripture is to encourage us to an awareness of and truthfulness about our tendency towards sin. It is also to teach us about our responsibility to hold one another accountable to "not sin", but if he or she does sin against us, to willingly, lovingly walk in forgiveness towards them. And we can do that because of our own tendencies towards sin.

Forgiveness is not just for the one who offends us. Forgiveness is also for the one who is offended. Without forgiving my offender, I am in as much bondage to the sin, as my offender. Jesus said it best. *"You have heard that it was said, `Love your neighbor and hate your enemy.' But I tell you: Love your enemies and pray for those who persecute you, that you may be sons of your Father in heaven... If you love those who love you, what reward will you get? Are not even the tax collectors doing that?"* (Matthew 5:43-46).

Really, deep within each of us is a desire to walk in love towards the other. And we want others to walk in love towards us. But because hurt people, hurt people, in their efforts to protect themselves from further pain, we are often become their victim. Hurtful experiences threaten our sense of safety and wellbeing. In turn, that makes us fearful of the intentions of others toward us. We then nurture and, to a large degree, cherish the feelings of pain inflicted upon us by the sins of others hoping to inoculate, or insulate ourselves from further pain. Or, in an effort to even the score and restore balance to our ego, we seek revenge. There is an old Chinese proverb that we would do well to remember, "The one who pursues revenge should dig two graves".

It is difficult to love anyone that you hold a grudge against. That is the personal imprisonment that results from unforgiveness. When Jesus said, "*Forgive us our debts, as we also have forgiven our debtors*" (Mt. 6:12), He was not only speaking about the ones who had offended, but also about those who had not made things right with those by whom offenses had come. We are not forgiven because we merely utter the words, 'I forgive', but because we have also, out of Christ's forgiveness towards us, chosen to make things right.

Two Greek words are used to translate the word forgive. The first is *charizomai*, from the word *charis*, which means "grace." This word means "to bestow a favor unconditionally; to show one's self gracious, kind, benevolent, or to pardon. The second word that is used to translate the word forgive is *aphiemi (ah-FEE-ay-mee)*[70] which means "to send away" or "let go." Clearly then, in this sense, forgiveness is not about the other person. It is about you – your freedom and release from what it does to you to hold on to unforgiveness.

I do not suggest to anyone that forgiveness comes easily. But the more you press into an understanding of the grace of God in your life, the more open you become, the more aware you become of that same grace at work in the life of the other.

It is that grace that will enable you to journey in the direction of true, authentic forgiveness. For most of us, forgiveness will not be an instantaneous action, it will be a process. It will be a process of the sanctifying work of the Holy Spirit moving us to greater compassion for those who sin against us, because of our humbling awareness of our sins against Christ – and yet He forgives. So as we live by faith in Christ, we forgive by faith in Christ.

How do I forgive?

1. **Acknowledge** that you have been sinned against. Forgiveness is not pretending; it is

---

[70] Strong's Exhaustive Concordance Strong's Number: 863

applying the balm of God's love to the scarred tissue of sin.

2. **See your offender as God sees them.** They are broken and in need of the Father's love. In their brokenness their motives of self protection resulted in sin against you – they hurt you.

3. **Do not minimize their sin, their wrong, but remember it is not in your power to get even.** God will judge all sin, but the desire for vengeance creates an additional sin burden for you.

4. **Remember God's grace when you have sinned.** See your offender as in need of the same grace that you ask of the Father on your behalf when you have sinned.

5. **Bring them before the Lord and ask God to move in the broken places of their life, that they may cease from sin and turn to His love.** He is a loving and forgiving God. Your prayers, on their behalf – your intercession, will do more for them and for you than any form of revenge you could devise.

Life Application

Extending forgiveness is a necessary step in the process of healing deep wounds. For most, it is the culmination of the intense work of revisiting and re-entering places and situations that have been the source of wounding in your life. If you have experienced opposition to the process and a reluctance to give up the defenses that you have nurtured to protect you from further injury in particular areas, I want to challenge you to contend for more openness. Hold tenaciously to the truth that God has spoken to you. He that has begun a good work in you will continue. Just know this, unforgiveness does not protect us from harm nor does it make another pay for what they have done to us. Equally, it takes energy and work to recall and to hold on to the emotions that keep forgiveness at a distance.

The text of Matthew 18:21-35 paves the way to our understanding about the power and importance of forgiveness. In this text we learn what forgiveness looks like and the penalty – the consequences of unforgiveness. Summarizing this parable of "the unmerciful servant" we learn we are able to forgive because we have been forgiven so much more. The passage does not limit forgiveness to 490 times, but to an unlimited number. Simply explained, seven is the perfect number, the number of completion. Using seven times seventy to demonstrate the perfectly limitless extent of grace filled forgiveness, Jesus teaches us four things:

1. We need to continue to forgive those who wrong us.

2. Forgiveness is not contingent upon the other person admitting their fault or asking forgiveness.

3. Forgiveness is not based upon other's actions but upon our attitude.

4. No matter how bad the things are that others might have done to us, we forgive them because God forgives us – despite the fact that the sin we have committed against God is still much greater.

We are commanded to forgive and sometimes that is a hard command to obey, simply because we confuse forgiveness with tolerance. You can forgive an offense or sin against you, but you are under no obligation to tolerate offenses purely because you forgive them.

Your healing begins when you forgive, but tolerating repeated offenses only subjects you to greater hurts in the long run. In such cases, you may need to sever that relationship. Yet, in giving the gift of forgiveness we ourselves are healed. As you look at your life there are some critical elements, about "what forgiveness is", and "what forgiveness is not", that you must keep in mind. You would do well to learn these truths.

What Forgiveness is:

- **Moral:** It is a response to an injustice, a moral wrong. It is a turning to the "good" in the face of this wrongdoing.

- **Goodwill:** Merciful restraint from pursuing resentment or revenge. Goodwill involves generosity. It is offering good things such as attention, time, and remembrances on holidays. It is an act of moral love, contributing to the betterment of the other.

- **Paradoxical:** While it is the foregoing of resentment or revenge when the wrongdoer's actions deserve it, forgiveness is also giving the gifts of mercy, generosity and love when the wrongdoer does not deserve them.

- **It takes us beyond duty:** A freely chosen gift rather than a grim obligation, it is the overcoming of wrongdoing with good.

What Forgiveness is not:

- **Condoning:** Nothing that bad happened. It was only this one time. It won't happen again.

- **Condemning:** She/he deserves to know they have wronged me. "Forgiving" with a sense of moral superiority.

- **Forgetting:** Extinguishing a memory or event. That is a physiological and psychological improbability. Even when a fire is put out, you remember there was a blaze.

- **Denial:** Pretending that it did not happen, time passing or ignoring the effects of the wrongdoing does not diminish in anyway the impact of a wrong done to you.

- **Excusing:** The person did this because ... it wasn't really their responsibility. (Remember if the Mac truck hits you accidentally you are no less hit if it hits you on purpose)

- **Seeking Justice or Compensation:** It is not a quid pro quo deal – it doesn't demand compensation first. Nor does your being wounded grant you license to wound someone else.

- **Forgiveness also does not mean that you re-enter a relationship at the same level or in the same way as that relationship was prior to the offense.** Some relationships are toxic and so are some people. In this case you may have to draw new boundaries or redefine the relationship altogether for your emotional health. And in some instances you may not be able to reenter a relationship at all, but you can still extend forgiveness. Dr. Everett Worthington, Professor Emeritus at the Virginia Commonwealth University, Richmond, Virginia, and principal of the Forgiveness Institute, suggests a "Pyramid Model of Forgiveness". Using the image of the pyramid and the acronym

REACH he offers this paradigm as a way of engaging the forgiveness process.[71]

Pyramid Model of Forgiveness
Dr. Everett Worthington

Recall the Hurt

Empathize with the one who committed the hurt

Offer the **A**ltruistic gift of forgiveness
(Genuine, charitable, benevolent and unselfish concern for the welfare of others)

Make a **C**ommitment to forgive

Hold on to forgiveness

Recall the Hurt - When we are hurt, we often try to protect ourselves by denying our hurt….if we don't think about it, it won't bother us. Eventually, unforgiveness intrudes into our

---

[71] Worthington, Everett L 1998. *The pyramid model of forgiveness: Some interdisciplinary speculations about unforgiveness and the promotion of forgiveness.* In Dimensions of Forgiveness: Psychological Research & Theological Forgiveness, ed. Everett L. Worthington, Jr., pp 107-138. Philadelphia: Templeton Foundation Press.

happiness or we develop physical symptoms like ulcers. Recall the hurt as objectively as possible. Avoid railing against the person who hurt you, instead, admit a wrong was done to you and set your sights on its repair.

Empathize - This involves seeing things from another person's point of view, feeling that person's feeling and identifying with the pressures that made the person hurt you.

Altruistic Gift of Forgiveness - Empathy can prepare you for forgiving, but to give that gift of forgiveness, consider yourself. Have you ever harmed or offended a friend, a parent or partner who later forgave you?

Think about your guilt. Consider the way you felt when you were forgiven. Forgiveness unshackles people from their interpersonal guilt. Recall your own guilt. Develop the desire to give that gift of freedom to the person who hurt you.

Commit to Forgive - When we forgive, we might eventually doubt that we have forgiven. When people remember a previous injury or offense, they often interpret it as evidence that they must not have forgiven.

Make forgiveness tangible - tell someone you have forgiven them

Holding onto Forgiveness - Painful memories DO NOT disqualify the hard work of forgiveness that you have completed. Remind yourself with positive thoughts about the forgiveness you have experienced. If you still struggle with the issue, work through the steps again.

In *The Art of Forgiving: When You Need to Forgive and Don't Know How*, Lewis B. Smedes tells us, "Forgiving does not erase the bitter past. A healed memory is not a deleted memory. Instead, forgiving what we cannot forget creates a new way to remember. We change the memory of our past into a hope for our future." Continuing he writes, "Forgiving does not usually happen at once. It is a process, sometimes a long one, especially when it comes to wounds gouged deep. And we must expect some lapses...some people seem to manage to finish off forgiving in one swoop of the heart. But when they do, you can bet they are forgiving flesh wounds. Deeper cuts take more time and can use a second coat."[72]

---

[72] Smedes, Lewis B. 1997. *The Art of Forgiving: When You Need to Forgive and Don't Know How.* New York: Ballentine Books

Dr. Worthington suggests there are three types of forgiveness that will help us to find freedom as we trust Christ for our healing. [73]

> **Decisional forgiveness** is a judicial statement that closes the books on the case. It says, "Case Closed." It means I have made a willful decision to no longer seek revenge nor to extract anything from the offender (like an apology or remuneration). Matthew 6:12-15.
>
> **Emotional forgiveness** is a process rather than a point-in-time decision. It is a process of allowing the Lord to bring you to the place where "replacing negative unforgiving emotions with positive other-oriented emotions like empathy, sympathy, compassion and love."
>
> **Interpersonal forgiveness** means forgiving yourself or forgiving another person, such as a spouse, who you are in an ongoing interpersonal relationship with.

What about forgiving God? Forgiving God! I am sure some may find the idea of forgiving God offensive. In some instances you may need to forgive God. Even in the scriptures, Jeremiah and other prophets held resentment toward God. When God punished his chosen people Israel, and Judah, for the sins and evil they committed, the prophets believed

---

[73] Op.cit.

that the punishments often seemed worse than the crime. For that reason, they resented God.

Forgiving God may seem unnecessary because God does not need your forgiveness. God acts with righteous judgment despite what you may feel about His actions. However, If you hold some deep resentment or even hatred against God because of some situation you believe He could have rescued you from, you, in a very real way, blame God for your malady. Even situations resulting from evil in the world that cause suffering, things that we label "acts of God", even these things can construct barriers that keep God at a distance. And when they do the pain that such situations create for us can lead to deep resentment.

So is there ever a need for you to forgive God? The answer maybe yes, if your resentments toward God are the result of your being hurt in situations where you believe God to be responsible. If looking deep within yourself you find you hold resentment towards God, you need to be reconciled with God. To be reconciled means "to become friends". God is reconciled to us. He did this through Jesus Christ and His finished work on the Cross. However, reconciliation works both ways. Both parties are to be conciliated to each other. First, God through Christ is conciliated to us, then we must be conciliated to God. This is where "forgiving God" comes in – you want to be reconciled, you want to be God's friend. It begins with forgiveness.

Christ wants us free. Forgiveness offers us the pathway to freedom. As you revisit all that God has done for you, you envision that person who has injured you as someone in need of the compassion and love that Christ as given you. You may not be able to reenter the relationship in the same way, but you can extend them genuine forgiveness and release them so that you can be free.

The Bible is very clear about sin (Romans 3:10, 23) and that there are consequences to sin (John 3:36, Romans 6:23). Forgiveness is not the refusal to acknowledge wrongdoing. It is not turning a deaf ear, or looking the other way – as if pretending will nullify sins effects. Jesus demonstrates the value He places on forgiveness throughout the scriptures. In the story of the woman caught in adultery, who obviously engaged in this behavior to meet a deep need. Her core longing for love, unaddressed caused her to turn to a dysfunctional behavior that could have cost her life. She escaped being stoned to death, because of Jesus' compassionate intervention. He knew that it was not about the sin, but about the deep need of her heart. Jesus used this occasion to teach a powerful principle.

There are deep needs within all of us. Specifically, we all have a need to be loved, to be told that we matter to someone. We all have a need to belong. Our heart cries for that in a thousand different ways. In John Chapter 8, the Pharisees and scribes presents the sinner – caught in the act of adultery.

And according to the Law of Moses, she should be put to death.

In his response to their charges, Jesus writes in the sand, after which each of them turned, walked away in silence until no one was left. Jesus said to the woman, "Woman, where are those accusers of you? Has no one condemned you?" (John 8:10, NKJV). She answered: "no one remains to condemn me." Jesus replied: "Neither do I condemn you; go and sin no more" (John 8:11, NKJV).

I just have to believe that what Jesus wrote in the sand was all their dysfunctional behaviors, all the things that they had done, and perhaps were still doing, to meet deep need – to satisfy their core longings. Why? Because, we were created for relationship and out of our need to be loved and accepted, we pursue relationships that we believe will embrace us, support us and accept us. Sometimes these are not good relationships. They may be destructive and reckless. Yet, our sense of worth and value is tied into these relationships. Fearful of having nothing else, we cling to them tenaciously, even at the threat of being hurt more.

Good relationships help us to understand and to experience the fullness of the Father's love for us. When these relationships are fractured by sin we have an amazing opportunity to see the love of God at work "up close and personal". Forgiveness is the key to restoration. Forgiveness is active loving. We are worth that only because God so loved.

To grow in the journey, you must realize, whether others accept you or not, God loves you and demonstrated that love in the person of Jesus Christ. *"You are not loved because you are valuable. You are valuable because you are loved."* We matter just that much to the Father, and Jesus demonstrated the Father's love in that while we were yet in sin, Christ died for us.

May you grow more and more into the awareness of so great a love, and from this place may forgiveness flow from your heart as your response to this amazing gift of love.

Do not let the secondary emotion of anger keep you from the freedom that you deserve. Anger, undealt with, can lead to hatred. Anger is about a wrong done to you and it is okay to be angry over a wrong done to you. Hatred is another thing.

Anger is directed at a behavior. Hatred targets the person. That is wrong. In a Christianity Today article, entitled, *The Unnatural Act*, Phillip Yancey recalls insights about forgiveness gleaned from the life of Nobel Peace Prize laureate, Alexander Solzhenitsyn:

> Forgiveness is the only way to break the cycle of blame--and pain--in a relationship. It does not settle all questions of blame and justice and fairness...But it does allow relationships to start over. In that way, said Solzhenitsyn, we differ from all animals. It is not our capacity to

think that makes us different, but our capacity to repent, and to forgive.[74]

You have the power to repent and forgive. That is what it will take to break the cycle of blame, and pain. Healing is not always about getting better or getting over something. It is really more about letting go of all the emotional baggage that weighs you down and keep you from being your true self.

---

[74] An Unnatural Act, Christianity Today, 8 April 1991, 36. 3 June 7, 2001

Chapter Sixteen

Obedience and Death
The Way of the Cross

And being found in appearance as a man, he humbled himself and became obedient to death — even death on a cross!
Philippians 2:8 (NIV)

Christ, the perfect Son of God, teaches us, by his example, that we learn obedience through the things we suffer. The writer of Hebrews reminds us, "Although He was a Son, He learned obedience from the things which He suffered" (Hebrews 5:8). Christ learned obedience through the things he suffered, not because of sin, but to be in solidarity with us as an "older brother", as a high priest who can fully be sympathetic and empathetic with our brokenness. *"For we do not have a high priest who cannot sympathize with our weaknesses, but One who has been tempted in all things as we are, yet without sin"* (Hebrews 4:15).

Even His advent, His coming to the earth was an act of obeying His Father. Remember His words in John 14:31, "That the world may know that I love the Father, and as the Father gave Me commandment, even so I do." The Father's purpose was the cross.

And, it was Christ's obedience, through an ultimate display of love that brought him there. Now, it is at the cross that we are confronted with the power of that love and our disobedience.

Many Christians have a problem with obedience motivated by sacrificial love. This is true, more often than not, because they focus on obedience as law or rule, rather than living in the grace Christ secured for them in His obedience to God. In truth, it is not my obedience, but his obedience that brings me into unity with the Father such that even when my best efforts fail I am still held closely in His love. My disobedience serves as a reminder of just how much I need grace that flows from His love.

In our journey, we come face to face with all that distances us from the redeeming radiance of the cross of Christ. For as difficult as it often has been to acknowledge the emotional dissonance and the pain that drives us to unanticipated and unexpected behaviors and choices, I have concluded that our greatest failure is a failure of love. It is a failure to live in the grace that has been so lavishly poured out from the Cross. This is true not just for me, but for all who truly get a glimpse of what the finished work of Jesus is all about.

When I really think on the cost, the sacrifice, the bigness of God's gift in Jesus Christ, this alone is humbling beyond words. Overwhelmed with deep appreciation, only the words of a wonderful hymn come closest to describing the feelings that well up inside of me:

> And, can it be that I should gain,
> an interest in the Savior's blood?
> Died He for me who caused His pain,
> for me, who Him to death pursued?
> Amazing love! How can it be,
> that thou, my God, shouldst die for me?
> -Charles Wesley 1739

Gazing at the Cross, feeling the weight of amazing love, moves me to a place of understanding and security that puts so much of the journey into perspective. There is a call to obedience in this journey. It is a call to the Cross. And the cross is the place where we say, "Not my will, but thine be done."

In African American spirituality there has always been a deep resonance with the sufferings of Christ and the resurrection hope. The imagery of the cross and resurrection evokes deep emotional responses, especially within the black worship experience. Christ's victory – the Cross, instills a tremendous sense of hopefulness that there is a victory to be had even in this life, if we trust his word and live it faithfully. Christ is the example.

Liberation theologians focus on our kinship with Christ as one who was oppressed as African

Americans have been and in so many ways still are oppressed. Our connectedness is to His poverty and pain because it so resembles the poverty and pain of the African American experience. So it stands to reason that His victory, seen in the triumph over the cross, inspires and stirs the African American soul with an incredible sense of blessed hope – victory shall be mine. Embodied in this victorious hope is the "Good News" – the Gospel, that authentic Christianity transcends race and ethnicity. The Good News firmly plants us into the reality that we are all God's children, created in God's image – stamped, imprinted by His blood and that is our true identity.

The Good News is that when the Cross of Christ is lifted high, all humanity bows, in recognition of one immutable truth, we are all made in the image of God, sinners in need of the redemption that only He freely gives.

To let go of cherished offenses, to surrender my pain and to no longer nurse present hurts is to fully obey and to follow in the footsteps of Jesus, whose image I bear, and whose heart I desire. It is to trust that I am, everyday, being transformed into his likeness with ever-increasing glory. Is this not the victory of the Cross? That in Christ's obedience, that which was meant to stamp shame and disgrace on all creation became the ultimate symbol of victory.

For the Romans the cross was the ultimate symbol of death and punishment, but the sacrificial death of Jesus on the cross for our sins redeemed that which was meant as a symbol of punishment and death, transforming it into a symbol of life and hope. The Apostle Paul writes,

> *And you, being dead in your trespasses and the uncircumcision of your flesh, He has made alive together with Him, having forgiven you all trespasses, having wiped out the handwriting of requirements that was against us, which was contrary to us. And He has taken it out of the way, having nailed it to the cross. Having disarmed principalities and powers, He made a public spectacle of them, triumphing over them in it.*
> *Colossians 2: 13-15*

The Cross of Christ – the Lord's Cross, the defining act of love, is the most supreme victory banner. And, just as Christ had to die to secure that victory, so too, must I die.

Mine is a death to self. It is a death that reconciles my desire to get even, for revenge, or even for retribution with the price that I could not pay for my sin. My death calls me to live in the reality of my indebtedness. For as much as I may find in culture, those situations that are unjust and unfair, when I look at them through the lens of the cross all that cries out in me for justice dies. What is birthed in me, is love. The kind of love that does not excuse a wrong done, but understands that the wrong doer has failed to love. And I do not need to know why. I just need to understand that where there is a failure of love, evil is alive and well.

Obedience is a constant challenge. Yet I hear, echoing deep within me, God's Word… "if you will live with me, you must die with me" (2 Tim 2:11). This challenge of obedience is a call to come, and die – to strive for the Christlikeness that reflects a new heart, and a new mind. This does not happen overnight, nor does it happen with simply reading scripture, saying prayers, or even getting baptized. This death, this crucifixion of myself that calls me to die that I might live, finds its fulfillment in the breaking of my will.

But when I look at Calvary, and I see the Lamb of God who takes away the sins of the world, beaten, broken, bleeding and dying for me, I find the grace to die with him. In his death, He conquered death in all of its forms. In fact, He paid the final price for the wages of sin and now extends to all who come under the crimson flow of His Cross, the gift amazing love; the gift of forgiveness and the gift of eternal life. "So I'll cherish the old rugged cross, till my trophies, at last I lay down. And I will cling to the old rugged cross, and exchange it someday for a crown."[75]

---

[75] Bernard, George, 1912, *Hymn: The Old Rugged Cross*

Life Application

"For the message of the cross is foolishness to those who are perishing, but to us who are being saved it is the power of God" I Corinthians 1:18

The venerated African American theologian, James Cone, writes in his book, *The Cross and the Lynching Tree*, about the paradoxical relationship of Jesus' death on the Cross and the history of the lynchings of blacks in the south from antebellum through the twentieth century. He clearly articulates that it was faith in the Christ of the Cross that inspired African Americans to hopefulness about God's coming salvation. This hopefulness rested on one abiding fact. African American people were continually faced with the threat of death that led to despair. Jesus' death on the cross represented a similar paradox, and because the cross was a place of both, the agony of Christ's crucifixion, and the promise of God's presence in the midst of suffering was the grounding for a collective hope.

In that tumultuous season of our country's history a black man could be lynched for any number of reasons: for being a successful businessman; for looking at a white man as his equal; for looking at a white woman with lust or for simply talking up for himself if wrongly accused. Lynching was seen as "the moral and Christian responsibility of white men to protect the purity of their race by any means necessary".[76]

Blacks could not find justice for the wrong treatment suffered at the hands of a jury of the white man's peers which only included white men. It is out of this reality that much of our pain was born.

In Cone's theological dynamic, lynching has a synonymous allusion of crucifixion and it is out of that hermeneutic that the Cross somehow mitigates the harshness of the times. Therefore, blacks filled the pews of churches on Sunday morning. Cone writes, "The spirituals, gospel songs and hymns focused on how Jesus achieved salvation for the least through his solidarity with them even unto death."[77] He argues that, because suffering and death were so evident in the daily lives of black men and women, they identified intimately with the God of the Cross. Why? Because... "In the mystery of God's revelation, black Christians believed that just knowing that Jesus went through an experience of suffering in a manner similar to theirs gave them faith that God was with them, even in the suffering on lynching trees just as God was present with Jesus in suffering on the cross."[78]

Black Christians found the courage to bear their suffering because of their faith in the God of the cross. Meaning and hope; courage and strength, to

---

[76] Cone, James, H. 2011. *The Cross and the Lynching Tree, p. 7*. New York: Orbis

[77] Ibid,(p. 21)

[78] Ibid, (p. 21-22)

stand against hostile structures, was found when they caught just a glimpse of the Cross.

In our journey, He has given righteousness to us. It was not earned but given to us because of the cross. In spite of all we have come through, we are indebted to Christ because of the power of the Cross. The Holy Spirit has given vision to see beyond hopelessness to a place of healing and deliverance, and has sealed in our hearts an unshakable faith.

We look back and wonder, *"How I Got Over"* And we know, it was the faithfulness of God coupled with the sacrifices of many souls who believed that the God of the Cross was our God. Therefore, we must make it a habit to give thanks and submit ourselves everyday to God. Because of the Cross, each day we are gifted with another opportunity to find the healing and wholeness that we need – it does come from Christ. There may continue to be obstacles of culture that we must overcome. There may be barriers that are rooted in sins, and evils that we will continue to pray through, but we cannot miss where God is in all of it. He still meets us at the Cross. And as Cone writes in the final section of his book, "No gulf between blacks and whites is too great to overcome, for our beauty is more enduring than our brutality."[79]

---

[79] Op. cit, (p.166)

Celebrating the Victory of the Cross

We have learned that without the Cross, we would be in bondage, as slaves to sin. But by His atoning work instead of slaves, we are His dear sons and daughters. By adoption we can cry Abba! Father! (Romans 8:15). And because of the Cross, we do not have to justify our actions by works to maintain holiness. We can come to the Father, ask, and receive His forgiveness.

Celebrating the victory of the Cross, there are at least three things that we must remember in our journey forward:

1. Affirm that God has been good to us – that His grace has hovered over us, protecting us from dangers seen and unseen. Just looking back at our history alone, we see the signs of God's grace and faithfulness. For many African Americans the fact that we have made it this far is in and of itself, an act of God. No other people can tell the story that we tell. We have earned the right to sing, "We've come this far by faith, leaning on the Lord. We need to celebrate that.

2. As we have come into greater truth, we realize that our passion, self-will, desires and cherished sins must be turned over to Him – turned around by Him, if we are to find the healing we so desperately need. Much of what has created

pain for us cannot be changed. *You can't unscramble eggs!* But it can be redeemed – exchanged for something more glorious. In this we appeal to the Holy Spirit for help, changing our hearts that we may have His heart, changing our minds that we may have His mind, healing us where we can be healed, helping us with what can only be redeemed.

3. Position ourselves to receive more and more of the grace of God in Christ Jesus. This allows us to let Him work in our lives. And as He works, we can better strategize for how he can accomplish His kingdom work through us on the principle of unconditional love alone. No one is better suited for this mission than we are.

For all that you have learned about yourself, and for as much as you are more aware than ever before of how strong the Father's love is for you, hold dearly to the truth – the Cross is the demonstration of God's great love for you.

For God was pleased to have all his fullness dwell in him, and through him to reconcile to himself all things, whether things on earth or things in heaven, by making peace through his blood, shed on the cross. Once you were alienated from God and were enemies in your minds because of your evil behavior. But now he has reconciled you by Christ's physical body through death to present you holy in his sight, without blemish and free from

> *accusation--if you continue in your faith, established and firm, not moved from the hope held out in the gospel. This is the gospel that you heard and that has been proclaimed to every creature under heaven, and of which I, Paul, have become a servant.*
>
> *Colossians 1:19-23 (NIV)*

As you continue to grow in the journey, celebrate the victory of the cross! Looking deep within reflection reflect on the places where you have met God in wonderful and affirming ways; where you have experienced His healing touch on your life; where you have been stretched to lean into His love and trust Him more.

Celebrate Victory through Trust: How can you begin to trust God more as you reflect on your journey?

Celebrate Victory through Honor: How can you begin to honor God with your attitude and actions as you live into the many lessons that you have learned?

Celebrate Victory through Worship: What one breakthrough or kairotic moment can you thank or worship God for as you revisit your healing encounters with the Lord?

Celebrate Victory through Love: What one thing could you do today to show God how much you love Him for the gift of His grace and mercy to you?

Celebrate Victory through Obedience: What is the Lord revealing to you about yourself through this intense time with Him that will help you begin to obey Him even more?

Celebrate Victory through Praise: What place of freedom and healing will you declare with a chorus of praise for His deliverance, as He has continued to meet you in your journey?

Celebrate Victory through Prayer: *Pray the Victory Prayer often...*

Dear Heavenly Father, I pray this prayer in the power of the Holy Spirit. In the name of Jesus Christ, I bind, rebuke, cast out and bring to no effect, all spirits that exalt themselves against the knowledge of you. I bind and break all curses that have been spoken against me. I bless those who curse me, and pray blessings on those who despitefully use me. The Holy Spirit leads me and guides me today. I discern between the righteous and the wicked. I take authority over Satan and all his demons, and those people who are influenced by him. I declare Satan is under my feet and shall remain there. I am the righteousness of God in Christ Jesus.

Satan you are bound from my family, my mind, my body, my home, and my finances. I confess that I am healed and whole. And Father, I pray for the ministry you have for me. Anoint me for all you have called me to do for you. I call forth divine appointments, open doors of opportunity, God ordained encounters and ministry positions. I claim a hedge of protection around myself, spouse and children (names) throughout this day and night. I ask you God, in the name of Jesus, that you dispatch angels to surround me, my spouse and children today and to put them throughout my house and around our cars, souls and bodies. I ask this prayer in the name of Jesus. Amen.

For information about the Ministry of Healing and Training opportunities in African American Soul Care, contact:

The Healing Place
Center for Counseling and Spiritual Formation
8150 Walnut Grove Road
Mechanicsville, Virginia 23111
(804) 730-1348

www.healingplace.firstshiloh.org
email: Ahealingforyou1@aol.com